JN131008

ACADEMIA 杉田 米行 監修　　　　　　　　　　　　NO.**8**
SOCIETY

American Politics
from American and Japanese Perspectives

英語と日米比較で学ぶアメリカ政治

2nd Edition

山岸 敬和
Michael Callaghan Pisapia

著

大学教育出版

Preface
はじめに

山岸　敬和
Yamagishi Takakazu
(Taka)

　皆さん、こんにちは！　南山大学国際教養学部でアメリカ政治を教えている山岸敬和です（文中では「Taka」として登場します）。本書に関心をもっていただきうれしく思います。

　私はこれまで日本人学生を対象に英語でアメリカ政治を教えてきました。そしてその中で学生が途方もない苦労をしているのを見てきました（私も学生の頃同じ苦労をしました）。英語で文献を読むときに学生が陥りやすいのは、①語彙力が足りずに文章を理解できない、②内容が細かすぎて要点をつかめない、③実体験がほとんどないアメリカ政治について学ぶため表面的な理解で終わってしまうということです。

　本書はこのような英語でアメリカ政治を学ぼうとする人たちの苦労を、①アメリカ政治を理解するための重要な語彙に日本語訳を付ける、②各章のまとめを日本語で行う、③日本との比較の視座を入れる、この３つで軽減しようというものです。本書は、いわばアメリカ政治について日本語で書かれた文献と、アメリカ政治について英語で詳細に書かれた文献との橋渡しをするものであるともいえます。

　しかし、本書は大学の講義で良い成績をとるためだけのものではありません（笑）。これからの世の中で活躍していくために必要なものを身につけるための準備として本書を使っていただければと思います。

　少し前に楽天やユニクロなどが英語を社内公用語化とすることを発表したことは大きな話題になりました。日本企業はますます競争が激しくなっていくグローバル経済で戦っていくために、日本人だけでなく世界中から優秀な人材を登用しようとしています。ただ会社で日本語を話すことを求めていては世界から集めることができる人材は限られてしまいます。そこで日本人にも英語を話すことを求めようとするのです。

しかし、人、お金、アイディアが自由に国境を越えて行き来するグローバル化された世界では、英語をいわゆる「ペラペラ話す」だけではダメです。英語で読み、分析し、議論し、そして自分なりの考えを発信しなければなりません。そして最後の「自分なりの考えを発信する」というのが重要となります。それは他の人、社会、国の考えや文化を理解し相対化しながら、自分の考えを作り上げる作業です。人や情報が自由に飛び交う世の中で活躍しようとすれば、自分のオリジナルな考えを世界に発信していけるかどうかが重要になってくるのです。

本書がそのための一つのステップになってくれればというのが私の願いです。すなわちアメリカ政治の基本的な仕組みや歴史的発展を日本と比較しながら英語で学ぶことで、アメリカ政治のみならず政治・社会・歴史というものを英語で考え、英語で議論するための基礎を皆さんに作っていただきたいのです。

本書は、アメリカ合衆国ノース・キャロライナ州にあるウェイク・フォーレスト大学でアメリカ政治を教えているマイケル・ピサピア先生との共同作業で書かれたものです。彼の専門はアメリカ政治ですが、日本の事についても関心があり日米比較研究も行っている研究者です。彼と初めて会ったのは南山大学において4泊5日で行われた名古屋アメリカ研究夏期セミナーでした。私は彼にこれから世界で活躍していく日本人のために手助けとなるようなアメリカ政治の本を書きたいと相談し、彼は快くその主旨に賛同してくれたというわけです。各章の最後には彼が日本についての素朴な疑問に対して私が答える「Cross-Cultural Dialogue」というセクションがありますのでお楽しみください。皆さんだったら彼の疑問にどのように答えるのかを考えてみるのもいいでしょう。

本書の読み進め方ですが、直接本文には入らないで下さい。まずは目次の後についている「アメリカ政治を理解するための用語集」でどの程度単語を知っているかチェックして下さい。最低半分、理想的には全てを記憶してから本文に入ることをお勧めします。次に、各章の最初にある日本語の要約を読まずに英語の要約から直接スタートして下さい。それがスムーズに理解できるようでしたらそのまま本文に入ります。ちょっと難しいと感じたら日本語の要約に戻って下さい。日本語の要約は英語の要約の訳になっています。まずは単語から入ることをお勧めするのは、読んでいる時に分からない単語がある度に止

まってしまうと全体の流れがつかめなくなってしまうという私の経験からです。用語集にない単語で分からないものがある場合は、とりあえず意味を想像しながら先に進んで下さい。

　最後に、アメリカという国は、日本にとって良きにせよ悪しきにせよ大きな影響力を持った国といえます。そして、本文でも触れるように、アメリカは全てが「政治化（politicized）」された国です。アメリカ政治を理解できないと、アメリカという国が理解できないといえると思います。そしてアメリカの本質が分からないと、アメリカ人に我々の主張を理解してもらうこともできません。そういう意味でも、本書が多くの人の勉学意欲をかき立てる小さな一歩を提供し、さらには異文化理解力を高め、自分の意見を世界に発信する力の向上につながればと願います。

　なお、本書の増版に伴い、初版が出版された2013年以降の情報を基に内容の変更を行いました。

　2021年8月

山岸　敬和

〈似顔絵：久木田知子〉

Michael Callaghan
Pisapia
マイケル・ピサピア

Hello, everyone! This is Michael. I am very fortunate to have met Taka several years ago at an American studies conference at Nanzan University, and I am so pleased to have worked with him on this book. When my graduate school advisor at the University of Wisconsin, Madison, suggested that I apply to attend the conference, I immediately jumped at the opportunity, since I long had an interest in Japanese history and culture.

My grandfather had been to Japan and when I was in high school I read a political novel called Shogun by James Clavell, which is about a Dutch trader traveling around Japan in the 1600s during the Tokugawa Shogunate. The history and the exaggerated characters made me want to learn about the true history of Japan. When I went to Amherst College, I studied Japanese language, and I learned about a Japanese student who graduated from Amherst in 1870. He founded Doshisha University in Kyoto. At that time, my studies concentrated on political thought and social theory. Later, when I went to graduate school in Wisconsin, I began to study the political development of American public education. At some point in the next few years, I hope to do a comparative study of the education systems of Japan and the United States.

Taka's and my goal with this book was to write a concise study of American politics that covers all the topics that American students learn about in their college courses. This book has a similar table of contents to many textbooks sold in the United States, but it is unique in three very important ways. First, our goal was to cover the main shifts in American political history, and to present that history in an engaging way that is suitable for Japanese college students. Second, we believed that frequent comparisons to Japanese politics would help to explain the unusual nature of American politics. Finally, Taka and I wanted to invite students to listen in on the interesting dialogues he and I have had with each other comparing the political cultures of the United States and Japan.

We believe that the United States and Japan have a tremendously important relationship with each other. The cross – cultural dialogues at the end of each chapter are meant to engage Japanese students to explore that relationship. We hope that all the students who read this book will come away wanting to learn more about the constitutional origins of the United States and its political development over time. We hope the chapters lead students to think about how Japanese history, politics and policy contrast with American history, politics and policy. Ultimately, studying the politics of another country should move us to think critically about the politics in our countries, and to take pride in what is exceptional in it, while engaging us to think about how our political lives could be otherwise.

I invite any students of this book who have questions about American politics or who want to follow up on some of the themes raised in the cross – cultural dialogues to please get in touch with me by email (pisapimc@wfu.edu). My "office" is always open, and I would welcome a correspondence with you!

March 2013

Michael Callaghan Pisapia

American Politics from American and Japanese Perspectives
2nd Edition
英語と日米比較で学ぶアメリカ政治

Table of Contents
目　次

Keywords to Understand American Politics
アメリカ政治を理解するためのキーワード集

　本書を理解するために重要なもの、そしてその他のアメリカ政治関連の英語で書かれた文献を読む時に繰り返し出てくる語彙を挙げました。したがって本書の中のすべての用語がここにあるわけではありません。日本語訳は以下に記した以外にも存在しますが、ここでは本書を読む時に手がかりとなる代表的な訳を挙げました。したがって、どうしても意味が通じない場合は辞書で確認してください。本文をよりスムーズに読み進めるためには半分、できればすべてを記憶することをお勧めします。左にチェックボックスがありますのでまずはどの程度正解できるかチャレンジしてみて下さい。太字になっているものはアメリカ政治を理解するために特に重要なキーワードです。

✓	キーワード	意味
	abolish	破棄する
	abolitionist	奴隷制度廃止論者
	abortion	妊娠中絶
	accommodation	施設
	acquire	取得する
	act	法
	activist	活動家、実践主義者
	address	取り組む
	administration	運営、管理（Obama administrationと大統領名が前についたらオバマ「政権」と訳す）
	admire	賞賛する
	admit	認める
	advance	前に進める
	advantage	有利な立場
	advertisement	広告
	advocate	主張する
	affect	影響を与える
	affirmative action	アファーマティヴ・アクション（積極的差別撤廃措置）

✓	キーワード	意味
	affordable	価格が手頃な
	African Americans	黒人（blacksともいう）
	agenda	課題
	agree	賛成する
	Agricultural Adjustment Act	農業調整法
	agriculture	農業
	alliance	同盟
	all-out	総力をあげての
	ally	同盟
	alter	変える
	ambiguity	曖昧さ
	ameliorate	改善する
	amendment	改正
	Americanization	アメリカ化：アメリカの建国の理念の下に国家統合を図ろうとする動き
	ancestry	系譜、先祖
	ancient	古代の
	Anglican Church	英国国教会

✓	キーワード	意味
	antagonistic	相容れない
	anticipate	予想する
	Anti-federalist	アンタイ・フェデラリスト：合衆国憲法の州による批准過程で批准反対を唱えたグループ
	anxious	心配な
	appeal	上訴する、惹き付ける
	appoint	任命する
	approve	認める
	argue	議論する
	arrangement	解決
	arsenal	兵器
	article	憲法の中の条項（Article of Confederationは別項）
	Article of Confederation and Perpetual Union	連合規約
	articulate	はっきり言葉で表現する
	assassinate	暗殺する
	assembly	集会、組み立て
	assert	主張する
	assessment	評価
	Associate Justice	陪審判事（首席判事以外の判事）
	Atlantic	大西洋の
	attempt	試みる
	attention	注目
	attitude	態度
	authority	権威、権限
	automobile	自動車
	autonomy	自治、自立
	avoid	避ける
	balanced budget	均衡予算
	ban	禁じる
	banking	銀行業
	bargain	取引する

✓	キーワード	意味
	behavior	行い（voting behaviorは別項）
	benefit	恩恵を得る
	bicameral	二院制の（議会）
	big stick diplomacy	棍棒外交（セオドア・ローズヴェルト大統領の外交政策を指す）
	bill	法案
	Bill of Rights	権利の章典
	bipartisan	超党派の
	blacks	黒人（African Americansともいう）
	block	妨げる（block grantは別項）
	block grant	ブロックグラント、定額の助成金
	blue-collar	肉体労働の
	bolster	強める
	boost	高める
	Boston Tea Party incident	ボストン茶会事件
	boundary	境界
	bribery	わいろ
	buddhist	仏教徒
	budget	予算（balanced budgetは別項）
	bureaucracy	官僚制
	bureaucrat	官僚
	cabinet	内閣
	campaign	選挙運動
	canal	運河
	candidate	候補者
	capacity	能力
	capitalism	資本主義
	captain	大尉
	capture	とらえる
	cartoon	漫画
	case	訴訟
	casualty	死傷者

✓	キーワード	意味	✓	キーワード	意味
	categorical grant	特定補助金		collapse	崩壊する
	Catholic	カトリック教徒		collective action problem	集合行為問題
	caucus (in Congress)	コーカス		colony	植民地
	census	国勢調査		command	命令する
	central govern-ment	中央政府：アメリカの文脈ではfederal government が中央政府となる。本書ではNational government と同じ意味で使っている		commander-in-chief	軍の最高司令官
				commerce	通商
				commission	委員会
				commitment	かかわり合い
	centralize	中央集権化する		committee	委員会
	Chairman of Joint Chiefs of Staff	統合参謀本部議長		common	普通の
				common law	判例法（主にイギリス）
	chamber	議院		compensation	補償
	checks and balances	抑制と均衡（主に行政府、立法府、司法府の間のバランス関係のことをいう）		compete	競争する
				complexity	複雑さ
				comprehend	理解する
	Chief Justice	首席判事		**compromise**	妥協
	Christianity	キリスト教		compulsory	強制的な
	circumstance	状況		condemn	非難する
	citizen	市民		confederate	同盟（Confederate States of Americaは別項）
	citizenship	市民権			
	city council	市議会		**Confederate States of America**	南部連合国（南北戦争中に南部州が連邦を離脱して作った国家）
	civil	市民の（Civil Rights movementは別項）			
	Civil Rights movement	公民権運動		conflict	対立
				confront	対決する
	Civil War	南北戦争		confusion	混乱
	civilian	一般市民		**Congress**	議会
	civilize	文明化する		congressional staff	議会所属のスタッフ
	claim	主張する			
	clause	法律の条項		conquest	征服
	cloture	議論打ち切り		consensus	意見の一致
	coalition	連合		consent	同意
	coerce	強制する		**conservative**	保守的（ヨーロッパの「保守」とは意味が違う）
	coercive federal-ism	強制的連邦制			
				consider	考える
	coexist	共存する		considerable	多大な

✓	キーワード	意味	✓	キーワード	意味
	consistent	首尾一貫した		critic	批評
	consolidate	統合する		criticism	批判
	constituency	有権者		culminate	ついに……となる
	Constitution	憲法		currency	貨幣
	Constitutional Convention	憲法制定会議（現在の合衆国憲法の草案を作った会議）		curriculum	カリキュラム
				death penalty	死刑
	constitutionality	合憲性		**debate**	討論会
	constructive	生産的な		debt	負債
	consumer	消費者		**decentralize**	分権化する
	contest	争う		**Declaration of Independence**	独立宣言
	continent	大陸			
	Continental Congress	大陸議会（独立までの）		decline	低下する、断る
				default	不履行
	contract	契約		defeat	敗北
	contradict	矛盾する		defect	欠陥
	contribute	貢献する		defend	防衛する
	contributory	拠出制の		deficit	赤字
	control	支配する		definition	定義
	controversial	異論が多い		delegate	代表
	conviction	信念		deliberation	議論
	cooperate	協力する		demagogue	衆愚政治
	cooperative federalism	協力的連邦制		demand	需要、要求する
				democracy	民主主義
	coordinate	調整する		**Democratic Party**	民主党
	corporation	企業			
	corruption	腐敗		Democratic Party of Japan	民主党（日本）
	council	会議			
	counterpart	対応する物		deny	否定する
	county	カウンティ（アメリカの州内の行政単位）		**Department of**	……省
				departure	逸脱
	court	裁判所		dependent	扶養家族
	covenant	誓約		describe	述べる
	coverage	普及率		desegregate	人種差別を廃止する
	crime	犯罪		deserving	……に値する
	criminal justice	刑事司法		destructive	破壊的な
	criminalize	犯罪とみなす		deterioration	悪化
	crisis	危機		determine	決定する

✓	キーワード	意味
	devastation	荒廃
	dialogue	対話
	Diet	国会（日本）
	dignity	尊厳
	diminish	減少させる
	diplomacy	外交
	disability	身体障害
	disagree	意見が一致しない
	discourse	議論
	discretion	自由裁量
	discrimination	差別
	discuss	議論する
	disenfranchise	選挙権を剥奪する
	disorder	混乱
	disparity	格差
	disperse	消散する
	dispute	論争する
	dissent	異議を唱える
	distinct	目立つ
	distinguish	区別する
	distort	ねじ曲げる
	district	選挙区（district courtは別項）
	District Court (of federal court)	連邦地方裁判所
	disturbance	妨害
	diversity	多様性
	divide	分ける（divided governmentは別項）
	divided govern-ment	分割政府
	divorce	離婚
	document	書類
	dollar diplomacy	ドル外交
	domain	大名
	domestic	国内の
	dominant	支配的な
	doubt	疑い

✓	キーワード	意味
	draft	草案
	dual federalism	並列的連邦制
	duty	関税、義務
	dynasty	王朝支配
	economics	経済学
	economy	経済
	education	教育
	effect	影響
	effective	効率的に
	efficient	効果的に
	egalitarian	平等主義の
	elaborate	念入りに仕上げる
	election	選挙（primary election, midterm election, general election は別項）
	election	選挙
	Electoral College	大統領選挙人
	electoral system	選挙制度
	electorate	有権者
	elicit	引き出す
	eligible	資格のある
	elite	エリート
	emancipate	解放する
	emancipation	奴隷解放
	embargo	出入港禁止
	embarrass	困惑させる
	emperor	天皇（日本）
	emphasize	強調する
	employee	被雇用者
	enact	制定させる
	endure	持続する
	enforcement	執行
	engagement	関わり
	enlightenment	啓発
	enmesh	巻き込む
	enrollment	入学者数、加入
	entail	伴う

✓	キーワード	意味
	enterprise	企業
	enthusiasm	情熱
	enumerated power	明記された権限（expressed powerと同義）
	enroll	加入する
	environment	環境
	equality	平等
	establish	設立する
	ethnicity	民族性
	ethno-centric	自民族中心主義
	evidence	証拠
	exaggerate	誇張する
	exception	例外
	excessive of democracy	民主主義の行き過ぎ
	executive branch	行政府
	Executive Office of President	大統領府
	expansion	拡大
	expenditure	歳出
	experience	経験
	expertise	専門性
	exploitation	搾取
	expressed power	明記された権限（enumerated powerと同義）
	extinct	廃止する
	facilitate	促進する
	facility	施設
	faction	派閥
	factor	要因
	factory	工場
	fatal	致命的な
	farewell address	告別演説
	farmer	農業従事者（independent farmerは別項）
	fear	恐れ

✓	キーワード	意味
	federal government	連邦政府
	federalism	連邦制
	Federalist	フェデラリスト（合衆国憲法の州による批准過程で批准推進を行ったグループ）
	feudal system	封建制
	filibuster	議事進行妨害行為（上院における議論引き延ばし行為）
	finance	財政
	fire	解雇する
	fiscal federalism	財政的連邦制
	floor (in Congress)	本会議場
	foe	敵
	force	強制力
	foreign	外国の
	foreign policy	外交
	formation	形成
	formulate	考案する
	foundation	基礎
	Founding Fathers	建国の父（独立戦争に参加し、独立宣言、合衆国憲法の成立に貢献した人々の総称）
	Fourteen Points for Peace	十四か条の平和原則
	franchise	選挙権
	free state	自由州
	Freedmen's Bureau	奴隷解放局
	freedom	自由
	French and Indian War	フレンチ・インディアン戦争
	frequent	たびたび起こる
	frustrated	失望する
	function	機能
	funding	資金
	gender	性

✓	キーワード	意味
	general election	一般選挙（有権者が政党の候補者の中から選択を行う選挙。政党の候補者を選ぶ予備選挙（primary election）とは区別）
	generation	世代
	geographic	地理的な
	gerrymander	ゲリマンダー、自らの有利になるよう選挙区を変更すること
	Give Me Liberty, or Give Me Death	自由を与えよ、さもなくば死を（パトリック・ヘンリーによる独立戦争を支持する演説の中の言葉）
	government	政府
	governor	州知事
	Great Compromise	偉大なる妥協（合衆国憲法起草時における州に対する連邦議会の議席の配分をめぐる妥協の一つ）
	Great Depression	大恐慌
	Great Society	偉大なる社会（ジョンソン大統領による社会改革の総称）
	gridlock	行き詰まり状態
	gross domestic product (GDP)	国内総生産
	guarantee	保障する
	gun	銃
	handout	施し物
	hatred	憎しみ
	health care	保健医療
	hearing (in Congress)	公聴会
	heritage	遺産
	heterosexual	異性間の
	hierarchy	ヒエラルキー、階層性
	highlight	強調する
	hire	雇用する
	homogenous	同質的な

✓	キーワード	意味
	homosexual	同性間の
	horizontal	横の
	House of Representatives	下院(日本では衆議院)
	household	世帯
	identity	自分らしさ
	ideology	イデオロギー
	illegal	違法な
	immigrant	移民
	impeachment	弾劾
	imperial judiciary	帝王的司法
	impetus	勢い
	implementation	執行
	import	輸入する
	inaugural address	就任演説
	incapacity	無能
	incarceration	投獄
	income	収入
	incumbent	現職(大統領、議員など)
	independence	独立
	independent farmer	自作農民
	independents	無党派層
	industrial revolution	産業革命
	industrialization	産業化
	inertia	惰性
	inevitable	避けることができない
	inferior	劣っている
	inflation	インフレーション
	influence	影響
	informal	非公式な
	infrastructure	インフラ、基幹施設
	inheritance	相続
	injustice	不当
	innovation	革新
	insist	主張する

✓	キーワード	意味
	institution	制度
	intellectual	知識人
	interact	関係を持つ
	interest	利益
	interference	干渉
	international relations	国際関係
	internationalism	国際主義
	interpretation	解釈
	inter-state	州際（州をまたぐ）
	intervene	介入する
	investment	投資
	involvement	関与
	Iron Triangle	鉄の三角形（議会、官僚、利益関係の関係性を示す言葉）
	isolationism	孤立主義
	issue	争点
	Issue Network	イシューネットワーク政策の専門家の関係性を示す言葉）
	jeopardize	危うくする
	Jewish	ユダヤ人の
	judge	裁判官
	judicial branch	司法府
	judicial review	違憲立法審査権
	jurisdiction	管轄権、権限
	jury	市民から選ばれた陪審員
	justice	公正、司法
	justify	正当化する
	Keynesian economics	ケインズ経済学（ジョン・メイナード・ケインズによって主張された経済学）
	knowledge	知識
	labor union	労働組合（trade unionともいう（イギリス英語に多い））
	laissez-faire	レッセフェール、経済自由放任主義

✓	キーワード	意味
	law	法
	lawyer	弁護士
	League of Nations	国際連盟
	lean	傾く
	legacy	遺産
	legal	法的な
	legislative branch	立法府
	legislature	立法機関
	legitimate	正当な
	lessen	減らす
	liberal	リベラル（注：米と欧では意味が異なり、アメリカではより大きな連邦政府の権力を主張する考え）
	Liberal Democratic Party	自民党（日本）
	libertarian	リバタリアン
	liberty	自由
	Library of Congress	合衆国議会図書館
	life sentence	終身刑
	limited	限られた
	literacy	読み書きの能力
	living Constitution	動態的憲法
	logical	論理的な
	Louisiana Purchase	ルイジアナ購入（1803年のフランスからの領土購入）
	loyal	忠誠心が強い
	Main Career Track National Public Service	国家公務員総合職試験（日本：平成23年までの国家公務員第Ⅰ種試験に相当するもの）
	maintain	維持する
	majority	多数
	Majority Leader (in Congress)	多数党院内総務
	majority opinion (of court)	判事の多数が支持する意見
	majority party	多数党

✓	キーワード	意味
	maneuver	策略
	manipulation	ごまかし、巧みな操作
	manufacture	工場制手工業
	marginalize	社会から置き去りにする
	marital	夫婦の
	market	市場
	marriage	結婚
	martyr	殉教者
	mass	一般大衆
	massacre	虐殺
	massive	重度の
	maximize	最大化する
	mayor	市長
	meaning	意味
	media	メディア
	medical association	医師会
	medicine	医療、薬
	Meiji Restoration	明治維新（日本）
	memory	記憶
	mercantilism	重商主義
	merit system	能力、成績制
	middle class	中流階級
	midterm election	中間選挙（大統領選挙を伴わない議会選挙のことを指す）
	military	軍
	minimum wage	最低賃金
	minority	少数
	Minority Leader (in Congress)	少数党院内総務
	missionary diplomacy	伝導外交（ウッドロウ・ウィルソン大統領による外交政策を指す）
	mobility	可動性
	mobilize	動員する（war mobilizationは別項）
	moderate	穏健な

✓	キーワード	意味
	modern	現代
	modification	修正
	momentum	勢い
	monarchy	君主制
	monetary	通貨の金
	monetary policy	融政策
	monopoly	独占
	morale	士気
	Mormon	モルモン教徒
	motivation	動機
	multilateral	多国間による
	municipality	市町村（日本）
	murder	殺人
	Muslim	イスラム教徒
	National Aeronautics and Space Administration	NASA、アメリカ航空宇宙局
	National Convention (of political parties)	全国党大会
	National Industry Recovery Act	全国産業復興法
	National Institutes of Health	アメリカ国立衛生研究所
	National Security Advisor	国家安全保障補佐官
	National Security Council	アメリカ国家安全保障会議
	Native American	アメリカ先住民
	Navy	海軍
	necessary	必要性
	negative	後ろ向きな
	negotiate	交渉
	neighbor	身近な人
	neighborhood	地域
	neutrality	中立
	New Deal	ニューディール、新規巻き直し（フランクリン・ローズヴェルトが行った社会改革の総称）

✓	キーワード	意味
	New Federalism	新連邦主義
	No taxation without representation	代表なくして課税なし（独立革命の際に使用された言葉）
	nominate	指名する
	Northwest Ordinance	北西部条例
	obligation	義務
	obstruct	妨害する
	occupation	職業、占領
	officials	役人、官僚
	old-age	高齢者の
	opinion	意見
	opponent	反対者
	opportunity	機会
	oppose	反対する
	oppressive	抑圧的な
	organize	組織する
	originalism	原意主義
	outcome	結果
	out-of-pocket expenses	自己負担
	overturn	覆す
	Pacific Ocean	太平洋
	Parliament	議会（イギリス）
	parole	仮釈放
	participation	参加
	partisanship	党派心
	passage	可決
	patient	患者
	patriarchy	家父長制
	patriot	愛国的な
	patronage system	猟官制（spoils systemともいう）
	penalty	刑罰、反則金（death penaltyは別項）
	pending	懸案の
	permanent	恒常的な
	permit	許可する

✓	キーワード	意味
	perpetrator	加害者
	perplex	当惑させる
	personnel	人員
	persuade	説得する
	petition	請願
	philosophy	哲学
	plead	嘆願する
	Pledge of Allegiance	忠誠への誓い（アメリカ合衆国への忠誠の宣誓。連邦議会の会期もこれを行って始まる）
	polarize	二極化する
	policy	政策（public policy, domestic policy, foreign policy, policymakerは別項）
	policymaker	政策立案者
	political action committee	政治活動委員会
	political appointee	政治任用
	political development	政治の発展（権力関係の変化）
	political institution	政治制度
	political science	政治学
	political theory	政治理論
	politician	政治家
	politics	政治
	poll	投票、世論調査（Poll taxは別項）
	poll tax	人頭税（pollは別項）
	population	人口
	populism	ポピュリズム、大衆の利益を第一とする考え
	Populist Party	人民党
	portray	描く
	position	地位
	positive	前向きな
	potential	可能性
	poverty	貧困

✓	キーワード	意味
	power	権力
	practically	事実上
	precede	先行する
	precedent	先例
	precinct	管区
	precisely	明確に
	prefecture	県（日本）
	prerogative	特権
	Presidency	大統領の地位、任期
	President	大統領
	presidential system	大統領制
	prevail	広く普及する、勝る
	prevent	防ぐ
	previous	前の
	price	価格
	priest	聖職者
	primary	最初の、主な
	primary election	予備選挙
	Prime Minister	首相
	principle	原理、原則
	priority	優先すること
	prison	刑務所
	privilege	特権
	procedure	手続き
	process	過程
	production	生産
	profession	専門的職業
	Progressive Era	革新主義時代（20世紀初頭の社会改革運動が起こった時期）
	Progressivism	革新主義
	prominent	目立った
	proper	適切な
	property	財産
	proportional representation	比例代表制
	prosperity	繁栄

✓	キーワード	意味
	protect	守る
	protection	保護
	Protestant	プロテスタント
	prove	証明する
	provide	提供する
	provision	規定
	pseudonym	ペンネーム
	public opinion	世論
	public policy	公共政策
	public school	公立学校
	public servant	公務員
	publish	出版する
	punish	罰する
	purpose	目的
	pursue	遂行する
	puzzle	なぞ、問題
	qualification	必要条件
	qualitative	質的な
	quantitative	量的な
	quorum	定足数
	race	人種
	race to the bottom	底辺への競争
	radical	急進的な
	raise	上げる
	ratification	批准
	react	反応する
	reasonable	理にかなっている
	reasoning	推論の結果
	rebellion	反乱
	recession	景気後退
	reconcile	和解する
	Reconstruction	再建（南北戦争後）
	recover	回復
	redistribute	再分配する
	reelect	再選する
	referendum	住民投票

✓	キーワード	意味
	reflect	反映する
	reform	改革
	refuse	拒絶する
	regime	統治方式
	region	地域
	register	登録する
	regulation	規制
	relationship	関係
	relevant	関係のある
	relief	救済
	religion	宗教
	reluctant	気乗りしない
	remind	思い出させる
	remove	取り除く
	renewal	更新
	repeal	廃止する
	representative democracy	代議制
	reproduction	生殖
	republic	共和国
	Republican Party	共和党
	reputation	評判
	require	必要とする
	reserved power	留保された権限
	resident	住民
	resist	抵抗する
	resource	資源
	respond	応じる
	responsibility	責任
	restrain	抑制する
	retirement	退職
	retrenchment	削減
	retrospective	振り返ると
	return to normalcy	正常への復帰
	revenue	歳入
	revise	修正する

✓	キーワード	意味
	revolution	革命
	revolving door	回転ドア
	rhetoric	レトリック、効果的な言葉の使い方
	right	権利
	rivalry	対立関係
	role	役割
	rotate	循環させる
	royal family	王族
	rule	統治、規則、裁決
	Rules Committee	議事運営委員会
	rural	田舎の
	safety	安全
	same-sex marriage	同性間の結婚
	scheme	体系
	scholar	研究者
	school district	学区
	seat	議席
	secession	離脱
	Secretary (of department)	長官(例:Secretary of Agricultureは農務長官)
	Secretary of State	国務長官
	sectionalism	セクショナリズム、地域偏重
	security	安全、防衛(social securityは別項)
	segregation	人種間の分離
	select	選ぶ
	self-help	自助
	self-sufficient	自立できる
	Senate	上院
	separate but equal	分離すれども平等
	separation of powers	三権分立
	serve	仕える
	settlement	植民
	share	共有する

✓	キーワード	意味
	sharecropper	シェアクロッパー、物納小作人
	sign	署名する
	similar	似ている
	single parent	一人で子供を育てる親
	skeptical	懐疑的
	slave	奴隷
	slave state	奴隷州
	slavery	奴隷制
	social order	社会秩序
	social security	社会保障
	socialism	社会主義
	socialized medicine	社会主義的医療
	society	社会
	socioeconomic	社会経済上の
	sovereignty	主権
	Speaker	下院議長
	spending	支出
	spoils system	猟官制（patronage systemとほぼ同義語）
	spread	広まる
	stability	安定
	stabilize	安定化させる
	stagnated	停滞する
	stakeholder	利害関係者
	standing army	常備軍
	Standing Committee	常任委員会
	state	州：アメリカ合衆国憲法が成立するまでのstateは「邦」と訳されることが多い。アメリカ以外では「国家」を主に意味する
	State of the Union address	一般教書演説
	Statue of Liberty	自由の女神
	status quo	現状維持
	stereotype	固定観念

✓	キーワード	意味
	stimulate	刺激する
	stipulate	規定する
	strategy	戦略
	strike down	無効であると宣言する
	structure	形づける、構造
	struggle	奮闘する
	subcommittee	小委員会
	subject	臣民
	subsidy	補助金
	substantially	事実上
	substitute	代替
	suburb	郊外
	succeed	後任となる、成功する
	sue	訴訟する
	suffer	苦しむ
	suffrage	参政権
	suggest	提案する
	suicide	自殺
	Superintendent	教育長
	superior	優れている
	supplement	補足
	supply	供給
	Supreme Court	最高裁判所
	supreme law	最高法
	survivor	遺族、生存者
	sympathy	同情
	tariff	関税
	tax	税
	Tennessee Valley Authority	テネシー州流域開発公社
	tension	緊張
	term	任期
	territory	領域
	textile	織物
	theory	理論
	think tank	シンクタンク

✓	キーワード	意味
	Third Way	第三の道（クリントン政権の中庸な政策を指す）
	threat	脅威
	Three-fifths Compromise	5分の3の妥協（合衆国憲法起草時における州に対する連邦議会の議席の配分をめぐる妥協の一つ）
	threshold	境界
	Tokugawa Shogunate	徳川幕府（日本）
	trade	交易
	trade union	労働組合（主にイギリス英語。labor unionともいう）
	tradition	伝統
	trafficking	密売
	tragedy	悲劇
	trajectory	軌道
	transformation	変化
	transportation	運輸
	treat	扱う
	treaty	条約
	tremendous	途方もなく大きい
	troop	軍隊
	trust	トラスト、企業合同
	turnout	投票率
	tyranny	専制政治
	tyranny of majority	多数による専制
	ultimately	最終的には
	unanimous	全会一致の
	uncertainty	不確実性
	unconstitutional	違憲な
	undermine	悪化させる
	unemployment	失業（unemployment insuranceは別項）
	unemployment insurance	失業保険

✓	キーワード	意味
	unification	統一
	uniform	均一の
	unilateral	一方的な
	Union (Civil War)	北軍（南北戦争）
	unitary system	単一性
	United Nations	国際連合
	United States of America	アメリカ合衆国
	universal	国民全体に行き渡る（universal suffrage, universal health insuranceは別項）
	universal health insurance	国民皆医療保険
	universal suffrage	普通選挙
	university	大学
	uphold	支持する
	urban	都市
	vaccine	ワクチン
	value	価値
	various	さまざまな
	vertical	縦の
	veto	拒否権
	Vice President	副大統領
	victim	被害者
	victory	勝利
	vindication	立証、主張
	violate	そむく
	violence	暴力
	vision	理想の姿
	vocational	職業訓練の
	vote	投票
	voting behavior	投票行為
	voucher	商品引換券
	wage	賃金（minimum wageは別項）
	war mobilization	戦時動員
	warn	警告する

✓	キーワード	意味
	wealth	富
	weapon	武器
	welfare	福祉
	Western Hemisphere	西半球（ヨーロッパから見たアメリカ大陸の呼称）
	whips (in Congress)	院内幹事
	white supremacy	白人至上主義
	withdraw	撤退する

American Politics from American and Japanese Perspectives
2nd Edition
英語と日米比較で学ぶアメリカ政治

CHAPTER 1

American Revolution and the Founding
アメリカ独立革命と建国

　アメリカの連邦政府の形成過程は、その後のアメリカの政治システムの発展に影響を及ぼした。1770年代から1780年代にかけて行われたアメリカ合衆国の建国は、1860年代に徳川幕府が崩壊した後の新政府の形成とは大きくその様相が異なっていた。アメリカの独立戦争と明治維新の違いは、日米両国の政治システムが大きく異なるものになる要因となった。第1章では、アメリカ植民地でどのような政治的対立が存在し、どのような背景でアメリカ独立革命が起こったのかを述べる。

Washington talking command of the American army under the old elm at Cambridge (1908). Courtesy of the U.S. Library of Congress.

How the government of the United States was created affects the subsequent development of the American political system. Formation of the United States in the 1770s and 1780s and formation of a new goverment after the Tokugawa Shogunate ended in the 1860s, happened in very different ways. The American Revolution and the *Meiji Ishin* dramatically changed the political systems of their countries. This chapter describes what kind of political struggles took place in colonial America and what drove the American Revolution.

If you would like to understand the nature of the American Revolution, thinking about your own country is a good place to start. The American Revolution has been compared often to the *Meiji Ishin* because both overturned their existing political orders. But notice that *Meijii Ishin* is commonly translated into the Meiji "Restoration," not the Meiji "Revolution." According to the Oxford English Dictionary, revolution is "a forcible overthrow of a government or social order in favor of a new system." In Japan, the Tokugawa Shogunate was overthrown. But the succeeding ruler was the emperor who had originally given the Shogun the right to rule Japan. The first emperor began his rule about 2000 years ago and the imperial system has continued since then.[1] Therefore, what *Meiji Ishin* brought was a restoration of power to the oldest existing political institutions of Japan. On the other hand, in the United States, thirteen colonies revolted against their subjection to the British colonial system. Whereas the American Revolution resulted in independence from the English empire, monarchy and parliament, the Meiji Restoration resulted in the restoration and reformation of the Japanese imperial system.

American Colonies and Japanese Daimyo

The foundings of modern Japan and the United States are different in another way. In Japan, many domains, or *daimyo*, such as Satsuma, Choshu,

---

[1] There are many theories about the origin of the emperor system.

and Echizen were all under the governance of the Tokugawa Shogunate. Moreover, the domains had horizontal communication, with their people connected by kinship. Because of their kinship ties and their experiences being governed by the centralized authority of the Tokugawa Shogunate, there was a near consensus after the Meiji Restoration that the Japanese would be under a new, centralized government together. By contrast in the United States, when the thirteen colonies gained independence from Britain, many Americans were still unsure about what the new country they were forming would look like, and how unified and centralized its new government would be.

The origins of the American colonies of Britain and the Japanese domains differed in two key ways. First, the Japanese domains were very old, while the American colonies were relatively new. Great Britain established Jamestown in the current state of Virginia, the first permanent American colony in 1608 – five years after the Tokugawa Shogunate began – while the Japanese domains had already been in existence for many centuries. In contrast to the Japanese

Thirteen Colonies and Territory Westward (1970). Courtesy of the U.S. Library of Congress.

domains whose political identities were much older than the Tokugawa Shogunate, the early immigrants moved to the American colonies in an institutional vacuum far from the center of the political system in London.

Second, while the Japanese domains had formed over many centuries within a feudal system, the American colonies were created for commerce and for religious freedom, and they had more autonomy than their Japanese counterparts. In fact, each of the American colonies had different characteristics. For example, the Jamestown colony was created by the Virginia

Company of London in 1608. The Virginia Company was charted by King James I to find gold and promote trade. The Plymouth colony, which became part of Massachusetts, was created in 1620 by Puritans who left England to practice their Protestant religion free from the Church of England. The Pennsylvania colony was established in 1681 after King Charles II decided to give the territory to the Penn family, in order to clear his debt. In contrast to Plymouth, Pennsylvania was open to immigrants from many different Christian sects. While the thirteen colonies shared a vertical relationship with the King, they did not have an institution that connected them horizontally. The horizontal communication was also limited by the fact that the colonies varied in their economy, society, culture, religion, and even language.

The Effects of the French and Indian War

The French and Indian War (1754-63), a war between Britain and France and their allies among different Native American tribes in the North American continent, changed the vertical relationships between the American subjects and the British government, and it changed the horizontal relationships between the people of the American colonies. Britain won against France, but the cost of the war brought Britain into a financial crisis. To increase revenues to pay for the war debt, Britain introduced new taxes for sugar, pamphlets, stamps, and tea in its North American colonies. The British government believed that their subjects in the American colonies would accept the taxes as part of the cost of paying for the war, but many colonials were not happy about the new taxes and resistance arose.

The colonials were divided into three groups: loyalists who supported the British government, moderate patriots who opposed the new taxes but did not support a revolution, and radical patriots, who wanted the colonies to fight for independence from Great Britain. Loyalists tended to have strong ties with the King and British commercial interests, and generally formed the elite of American society. They had a tendency to support whatever the home country demanded, because the status quo benefitted them. Moderate patriots had more to lose from the new laws, but they believed that unfavorable laws could be challenged by asserting their claims as British citizens. Lastly, radical patriots had little to lose in social and economic status if they separated from Great Britain, and they argued that the British King and parliament cared nothing about the rights of colonial Americans. They claimed there was little hope that the British government would change its policy toward the colonies; instead, the colonies should cooperate with each other and work toward independence.

In 1773, the frustration with British policy led to the Boston Tea Party incident, when radical patriots dumped thousands of boxes of English tea into Boston harbor, rather than paying taxes on it. This event resulted in the increased popularity of radical patriots and their slogan, "No taxation without representation." Every American learns this slogan as a child: it captures the basic idea of the American Revolution – that citizens cannot be coerced to part with their property without having their voices heard in government. Though many in Massachusetts approved of the radical patriots, most Americans still did not want to break from England. When delegates met at the First Continental Congress convened in Philadelphia in September 1774, it was not to seek independence, but to prevent it from happening. The Congress decided to act against Britain by boycotting British products. They were still hoping that they could use peaceful means to pressure their home country to address their frustrations.

The Battles Begin

In April 1775, however, a gunshot was fired. Britain and the colonials began military conflicts outside Boston, known as the Battles of Lexington and Concord. The number of colonials who sought independence increased as patriots portrayed the battles as British violence against civilians. The Continental Congress gathered again in May to discuss how to pursue the war against Britain. Still, the idea of forming a United States that would be independent from Britain was not yet dominant. Many Americans enjoyed the privileges of being British citizens, and they thought of themselves as subjects of the British crown. Britain was a super economic and military power at that time. Being British subjects meant they were protected by Britain's power. Many colonists could not imagine themselves being citizens of an unknown, and probably very weak, country in the future.

In January 1776, frustrated with the inertia among the colonials, Thomas Paine wrote a pamphlet, titled *Common Sense*. He equated monarchy with tyranny and argued that it was not logical that a British King and parliament should control a big colonial territory that was physically far away. He also noted that the American colonies should create their own country based on the idea of a "Republic" because the world's inevitable trend for humanity was to enjoy liberty, not to be the subjects of tyranny. Paine's arguments spread throughout the colonies, and his ideas gave radical patriots ideological backbone. With his writings and the actions of the patriots, many colonials began to believe that independence from Britain would be unavoidable.

The Declaration of Independence

On July 4, 1776, six months after *Common Sense* was published, moderate and radical patriots signed the Declaration of Independence, written by Thomas Jefferson and edited by a committee of the Continental Congress. "The unanimous Declaration of the thirteen united States of America," stated:

> We hold these truths to be self-evident, that all men are created equal, that they are endowed by their Creator with certain unalienable Rights, that among these are Life, Liberty and the pursuit of Happiness. – That to secure these rights, Governments are instituted among Men, deriving their just powers from the consent of the governed, – That whenever any Form of Government becomes destructive of these ends, it is the Right of the People to alter or to abolish it, and to institute new Government, laying its foundation on such princi-

ples and organizing its powers in such form, as to them shall seem most likely to effect their Safety and Happiness.

The Declaration of Independence asserted that the new country would be very different from Britain. Drawing upon the enlightenment ideas of John Locke and other European thinkers who argued that individuals bear natural rights to life, liberty and property, the Declaration stressed that rights and ideas such as liberty, equality and democracy, not the privileges of monarchs and Lords would be the foundation of a new country.

Liberty meant being free from tyranny and having the freedom to exercise choices and accumulate property without interference from the government. Equality was the idea that all citizens have an equal

Americans celebrate the Independence Day with fireworks. Courtesy of Kanako Ishikawa.

right to consent to the government – not the idea that all people should enjoy equal amounts of property and success. This contrasted directly with the idea in British society of distinct social classes – a landed aristocracy and everyone else – that would have different privileges in society. Lastly, the idea of democracy meant that a large number of citizens should have the right to choose and change their leaders in periodic elections. However, the American elites did not support full suffrage rights for all citizens, as they believed this would result in government by demagogues. On one hand, they believed that the people should have freedom from too much government authority. On the other hand, they knew that government was a necessary evil: people would be worse off without some governmental protection, such as police and army power. The idea of elections in a limited democracy – that not all the people, but only the best citizens would vote and hold office – allowed for a government that was also controlled by the people.[2]

Many Japanese people, and many Americans, misunderstand two things about the Declaration of Independence. First, it was not a document to prove that colonies had gained independence; rather, it was a

"Reading the Declaration of Independence by John Nixon, from the steps of Independence Hall', Philadelphia, July 8, 1776. Courtesy of the U.S. Library of Congress

political document used to boost the morale among the people of the thirteen different colonies and move them to cooperate to fight against Britain and become independent. Americans did not truly become independent until the end of the Revolutionary war, when the Treaty of Paris was signed and Great Britain approved the independence of the United States in 1783. Second, it was not to declare that thirteen colonies would be independent and come together as one country. Although each colony sought its own independence, they issued a joint declaration because they knew a unified statement was more threatening to Britain than making thirteen separate declarations. The Declaration of Independence, therefore, did not say much about what kind of country or countries the colonies would become.

A New "Country" under the Articles of Confederation

While they were fighting against Britain, however, the thirteen states made the first attempt to create a country that was very different from the current United States. In 1777, the Constitutional Congress passed the Articles of Confederation and Perpetual Union. When the Americans won the war, the new country was governed by the Articles from 1781 to 1789 when a new constitution, the Constitution of the United States, was established. The union of states under the Articles was not a single nation or

---

[2] The term democracy itself is not found in the Constitution because it was considered as politics by mobs at that time.

country, but much more like a military alliance.

The Articles of Confederation did not give the national government much power. It reads, "Each state retains its sovereignty, freedom, and independence, and every power, jurisdiction, and right, which is not by this Confederation expressly delegated." This is the beginning of the tradition of "expressed and reserved powers," which claimed that the national government could do only what was written in the constitution, while all other powers not expressly listed were reserved to the states.

The Articles of Confederation limited what the Confederation Congress could do. It was allowed to declare wars, make treaties, issue coins, and regulate the value of coins and so on. But the Confederation Congress could not function efficiently and effectively because of two problems. First, it had difficulty in passing bills since it needed nine votes out of thirteen in the Congress. Second, it did not get authority to have a standing army and levy taxes. Therefore, even if the national government had declared a war, it would have relied on the state governments to supply arms. Lastly, the Articles of Confederation did not make an executive branch. The implementation of policies was put in the state governments' hands. The state governments strictly maintained their sovereign power.

A weak confederal government could not last long. Because each state set different tariffs, inter-state and international commerce did not develop well. Moreover, debtors became the majority in some state legislatures and they passed laws to make inflation and, even worse, to default on their debts.[3] Uncertainty about the American economy, society, and politics increased under the Articles of Confederation.

Some elites believed that giving too much power to the peoples of the different states led to an "excess of democracy." The Articles of Confederation allowed states to have sovereign power and the state legislatures in some states were controlled by popular majorities. This meant that political

---

[3] States had their own property requirements for voting rights. But because they were lower than ones in Britain, many white men, including financially weak ones, could vote.

power was much closer to the people than it would be if the Confederation government had more authority. That was a democracy the Articles of Confederation sought to create. But it appeared that that kind of democracy did not work and would tear the new country apart. The elites began to think that a new constitution would be needed to solve conflicts across state lines, and to give more power to the elite classes within each state, against the middle classes. Momentum to make a new constitution was triggered by a big event.

Shays' Rebellion

Shays' Rebellion (1786-87) was the critical event. In Springfield, Massachusetts, Daniel Shays led a rebellion against laws passed by the state legislature (called the General Court) in Boston. He saw that the ordinary people were suffering financially. The main goal of Shays' Rebellion was to abolish Massachusetts' flat poll tax that affected the poor much more than the rich. He served as a captain in the American Revolution and thought that life in the new United States was different from what he had imagined.

Elites in the United States were shocked not only by Shays' Rebellion itself, but also that the government of the Confederation could not effectively react to the rebellion. As written in the Articles of Confederation, the federal government did not have the authority to raise taxes and have a standing army. What the Confederation government could do was to ask state governments to cooperate. The limited capacity of state governments to control the rebellion frustrated national elites, including George Washington. He eventually led troops to end the rebellion. But the Shays' Rebellion traumatized many elites. They thought that the United States would become extinct with the weak national government of the Confederation. They wanted a stronger central government.

Shays' Rebellion resulted in a big push for the formation of the Constitutional Convention. It was convened in Philadelphia in May 1787, a few months after the Shays' Rebellion came to an end. Its goal was to discuss how to make a more powerful central government that could more effectively confront situations like Shays' Rebellion and other national crises. But to what degree the national government should have more power over the states was highly controversial.

Plans for the New Constitution

The initial motive of the Convention was to discuss problems of the Articles of Confederation and revise a few parts of it. But many, including James Madison who was later called "the Father of the Constitution," decided that they should draft a new constitution to make the national government stronger. Their idea soon prevailed. But they had to conduct a delicate task to create a stronger national government without advocating a radical departure from the spirit of the Articles of Confederation, based on the idea that the United States would still have a far more limited government than the governments of the European countries.

Madison and other Virginia delegates arrived in Philadelphia earlier than most other delegates. While they had to wait for the Convention to secure a quorum of seven states, they wrote down their ideas for a new constitution, which became known as the Virginia Plan.

Whereas the Articles of Confederation had established a single chamber legislature, the Virginia Plan proposed that the legislative branch should be bicameral, as it was in many state governments, and in the British parliament. Moreover, the Virginia Plan suggested that representation of the states in the new legislature should be based on their populations. This differed from the Confederation Congress in which each state equally had one vote, regardless of their populations. This proposal was shrewd. While it claimed that two chambers would help to make legislation a slower process based on greater deliberation, it also sought to make the legislative process more efficient by giving more power to the larger states, like Virginia, to control the agenda, and reduce the number of players who could block the agenda.

The Virginia Plan also called for the creation of three branches of government – legislative, executive, and judicial – whereas the Articles of Confederation had created one branch, a Congress with very limited executive and judicial functions. Madison argued that the three branches would check and balance each other, and thus restrain the power of the new national government. For example, the plan included a national executive who could veto acts by the legislative branch, and a judiciary that would have jurisdiction over cases dealing with the collection of national revenues, and with the impeachment of national officials.

The Virginia plan was presented at the beginning of the Convention. Delegates from the smaller states soon opposed it because they disagreed with the principle that representation of states in Congress should depend on the size of the population. They formulated the New Jersey Plan because they believed that the Virginia Plan would lessen their political power in the new Congress. They wanted to leave the structure of Congress the same as it was under the Articles of Confederation, with a single chamber in which each state would have the same number of representatives in the Congress. Like the Virginia Plan, the New Jersey plan also created an executive and a judiciary, but it tried to make them weaker than the legislative branch.

Compromises to Create the Constitution

The conflict between supporters of the two plans was reconciled in the Great Compromise, proposed by the delegation from Connecticut. The Great Compromise was to create a bicameral Congress in which the states would have an equal vote in the upper house, or Senate – an idea that pleased supporters of the New Jersey Plan. On the other hand, representation in the lower chamber would be based on the population in the states, as supporters of the Virginia Plan had wanted.

Independence Hall in Philadelphia where both the Declaration of Independence and the U.S. Constitution were discussed. Courtesy of Saemi Yabushita.

Another conflict emerged over how to determine how many seats each state would have in the new House of Representatives. Delegates disagreed about how to count the population of each state, given that many people in the South were slaves, but under the law, slaves were a form of property, not citizens. Delegates from Virginia and the other Southern states insisted that slaves should be counted fully as part of the population to increase their political power in Congress. Delegates from Free states, such as New York and the other northern States claimed that slaves were considered as personal property, not people. And since they were not citizens, they should not be counted for purposes of representation.

Again, a compromise was made without which the new constitution could not have been formed. This is called the "Three-fifths Compromise": the delegates wrote into the Constitution that five slaves were to be counted as three people. These two compromises helped the delegates of all states – whether big or small and whether slave or free – agree on representation in the new Congress, the key branch of government established by the new Constitution.

Besides the controversies about the legislative branch, there was a heated debate about the structure and role of the new executive branch. An executive branch controlled by a single person reminded many Americans of the oppressive power of the British King. However, many delegates at the Convention understood that the executive branch would be necessary to make quick decisions on certain matters, such as military actions, and to prevent the legislative branch from

Benjamin Franklin, the eldest among the delegates, played an active role in making the new Constitution. Courtesy of the U.S. Library of Congress.

being a tyranny of the majority.

However, nobody wanted the executive branch to be a tyranny, either. Worrying about the birth of tyranny in the United States, delegates who supported the New Jersey plan suggested that a multiple person council lead the executive branch. This plan was rejected, and instead, the delegates concluded that one person would head the executive branch. While he would be powerful in many respects, as commander-in-chief and as chief executive in the implementation of policies, his power would be strictly balanced by the other branches (see Chapter 2).

On September 17, 1787, the Constitution of the United States was signed by delegates at the Convention. But their approval was not the end of the process. The Constitution had to be ratified by the people of each of the states in special conventions. The state conventions would meet specifically to consider whether ratification was a good idea. It appeared to the signers, however, that the ratification process would not be easy. They saw that some delegates left the Convention dissatisfied, and three delegates present at the Convention refused to sign it. Moreover, two prominent signers of the Declaration of Independence, Samuel Adams and Patrick Henry did not even come to the Convention because they opposed the idea of a stronger national government that the Convention had organized to make a reality. Supporters of the new constitution had to convince the public that it would not be a threat to the several states and that it would in fact lead to "a more perfect union."

Cross-Cultural Dialogue 1:
Imagining the National Origins of Japan and America

Michael : "When I was growing up in the 1980s, my friends and I were fascinated by samurai culture because of a silly role playing computer game we used to play. In the game, you would start out as Lord of a daimyo and work your way up to try to become *Shogun*, and create a lasting dynasty. We found the game very exciting: using military power and honor and sometimes treachery to create peace. But, I've always wondered what the Tokugawa Shogunate means to the Japanese today. For most Americans, American history begins with the Revolutionary war, with the fight for freedom and independence from England. That's also the beginning of American national identity. Where does Japanese history begin, and how is that origin different from the American founding?"

Taka : "I think I played the same game when I was a kid. It was fun! For Japanese, the Meiji Restoration is definitely not the beginning of our country's history. Kids start to learn about Japanese history from the ancient times, often from the Jomon period starting more than 10,000 years ago. Many people are fascinated by the history before the Meiji

Restoration. Recently, another history learning boom has come and it is interesting this time because more women are showing a strong interest. These women are called *rekijo*, or "history women" in English. I think that many Japanese people like the pre-Meiji Restoration history because they find their roots, in other words their Japanese-ness, in the historical events and people. For Americans, the American Revolution is the beginning of the history. But for Japanese, the Meiji Restoration is merely a historical event to change the ruling system, not an event to make a new country."

CHAPTER 2

Principles of the U.S. Constitution
アメリカ合衆国憲法を支える理念

日本国憲法第98条もアメリカ合衆国憲法第6条も憲法は国家の最高法である
と規定している。しかし、アメリカ人にとっては合衆国憲法というのは国を治
めるための最高法であるという以上の意味を持っている。それは国家の象徴で
ある。また13の州が新たな国家を形成する時の契約であり、現在においても50
州の人民を一つ国家として束ねるものである。憲法はアメリカ人にとって国の
歴史そのものであるといえる。第2章では、合衆国憲法を支える主な政治的理
念、権利の章典、そしてその他の憲法修正条項について論じる。

Signing of the U.S. Constitution in Philadelphia. Courtesy of the U.S. Library of
Congress.

Both Article 98 of the Japanese Constitution and Article 6 of the American Constitution say that the Constitution is the supreme law of the nation. But to the American people, the American Constitution is more than a legal document laying out the highest law of the land. It is a symbol of the nation. It was a contract for the thirteen states to make a new country and is still a contract that weaves the people of the 50 states today together into one national fabric. It is the history of the country itself. This chapter discusses the major political principles underlying the Constitution, the Bill of Rights and other important amendments.

As Chapter 1 described, the Articles of Confederation was the first attempt by the thirteen states to maintain their sovereignty, coexist and survive. When the founding fathers realized the Confederation was not strong enough, they started to draft a new constitution. They sought to create a constitution that would protect the nation from the dangers of excessive democracy, and from internal and international disturbances. With many compromises among delegates, the Constitutional Convention produced a new constitution. But its ratification process was expected to be uncertain.[1]

Patrick Henry and Samuel Adams who refused to participate in the Constitutional Convention were among those who opposed the new constitution. Henry was famous for his words, "Give me Liberty, or Give me Death," which encouraged the movement toward American independence. He strongly believed that states should maintain their sovereign power and that the new constitution would lead to the birth of a new tyranny.

Advocates of the new Constitution had to convince the public that it

---

[1] Neither the Imperial Constitution nor the Japanese Constitution needed to be ratified by the prefectures. The importance of ratification in the American states is a good example of the principle of federalism at the heart of the Constitution. By contrast, Japan is based not on federalism, but on a unitary system. See Chapter 4 for an extended discussion of American federalism.

would not cause harm and would bring a better condition to them and the country. They were called the Federalists and their opponents were called the Anti-Federalists. The Federalists included James Madison, Alexander Hamilton and John Jay. They used the pseudonym Publius for a serial of 85 articles published in the newspapers of New York, where political elites were very reluctant to ratify the constitution. These articles are now called the Federalist Papers. The Anti-federalists also published many papers, hoping to sway delegates at the state conventions to reject the new constitution. One of the most influential, Robert Yates, a good friend of George Clinton, the governor of New York at the time, used the pseudonym Brutus for the essays he published. Just as the ancient Roman Brutus had taken the life of Julius Caesar in order to prevent the Roman Republic from becoming a tyranny and empire, Yates hoped his essays would move Americans against the newly drafted Constitution, which he believed was a real threat to their liberties.

Ideas about the Constitution in the Federalist Papers

The arguments in the Federalist Papers ultimately prevailed and for two centuries now, the Supreme Court has cited them as the Founding Fathers' interpretation of the constitution. Madison, Hamilton and Jay argued that the new Constitution would solve the problems under the Articles of Confederation and make the country stable and stronger. These papers do an exceptionally good job of defining the principles of the new Constitution, and all students of American politics should have a basic understanding of them.

Federalist No. 10 by James Madison argued that a larger country or a "Great Republic" would do a better job than any single small republic could do of preventing one faction in society from dominating the rest of society. Madison was concerned that a majority of a state's residents, who are middle class or poor, would form a majority and control the government at the expense of the upper classes. He worried about this because the state legislatures suffered from excessive democracy – often under the control of debtors. The best way the minority in a state could be protected against a majority faction, he argued, was to enlarge the total number of factions in the whole republic. Establishing the new Constitution would do this. His logic was that by multiplying the number of factional interest groups, you could create a political universe where all of them worked against one another, so that no single faction controlled all things. Political scientists today refer to this view as pluralism. Moreover, Madison argued that the direct election of members of the House of Representatives and indirect election of Senators by the state legislatures would allow the federal legislature, or Congress, to reflect a greater variety of interests or factions. Again, this would help to limit the power of the new national government.[2]

Federalist No. 39 by Madison described what kind of nation would be created by the new Constitution. He argued that the new national government would be a republic, but a new kind of republic that the world had never seen. The American republic, according to Madison, would guarantee that the governing power would be derived from the people, that elections would be a tool to choose leaders, and that leaders would have to maintain good behavior during their terms in office. Responding to the Anti-Federalists, who suggested that the new Constitution would abolish the federal character of the Union, Madison argued step by step how the Constitution was national in some respects, and federal in others. First, he pointed out how the ratification process itself, which requires that the states must agree to the Constitution before it has legal force, reflects the federal principle. Second, he considered the Congress: whereas representation in the House is meant to reflect national majorities – a national principle – representation in the Senate is meant to reflect the sovereign voice of each of the states – a federal principle. Third, he pointed out that the President is supposed to be a representative of the entire nation, on the one hand, and on the other that the complex process of selecting the president

---

[2] Senators used to be elected by the state legislatures until the seventeenth amendment to the Constitution, established in 1913.

through the Electoral College reflects a principle of federalism (see Chapter 6). Finally, Madison indicated that the amendment process laid down by the Constitution is based entirely on the principle of federalism: in order for the Constitution to be changed, not only does Congress have to approve an amendment by supermajorities in the House and Senate; in addition, 3/4 of the states have to ratify it. Such a high threshold means that a very small number of states can block a major change to the national framework – a plain reflection of how the Constitution would reflect the interests of the several states.

Federalist No. 51 is the most famous of the Federalist Papers. In it, Madison emphasized again that a stronger national government would be needed to maintain the stability of the republic. While the main purpose of the essay was to explain how the new government would not become a tyranny, he used the opportunity to present a pessimistic view of human nature: "If men were angels," Madison reasoned, then "no government would be necessary." But, once a people set up a government to protect men from one another, they needed to make sure that they also set up institutions that would prevent the government itself from becoming too powerful. Here, Madison in effect argues that the framers of a constitution have to work with the material they have: if men are self-interested and ambitious and are not like angels, then it makes sense to harness that self-interest to ensure that the "ambition" of one man in office will counteract the ambition of others.

Again, as in Federalist 10, Madison's main idea is that having inter-ests push against each other is the best way to protect any single interest from becoming dominant. In order to make sure that each official had differ-ent ambitions, he argued that officials should be selected through different channels coming from the people – that is, by different electorates and sys-tems of appointments. So, he stressed how the new Constitution introduced a separation of powers that prevented one branch in the national govern-ment from having all the power. "Each department," he wrote, "should have a will of its own; and consequently should be so constituted that the members of each should have as little agency as possible in the appointment of the members of the others." The will of the officials in each department would be different because the officials are elected by different constituencies: the President, by a national electorate; the Senators by state legislatures; and members of the House by the electorates of the many Congressional districts.

Finally, Federalist No. 78 by Alexander Hamilton supplemented Madison's argument about the separation of powers. Hamilton believed that an independent judicial branch was necessary for monitoring the constitutionality of what the legislative and executive branches were doing. The Anti-Federalists were especially worried about this branch of government, composed of unelected judges who were allowed to have lifelong tenure. What purpose, they wondered, could such a judiciary play in a republican

Alexander Hamilton, born in a Caribbean island, strongly believed that the strong central government would be necessary to save the new country. Courtesy of the U.S. Library of Congress.

form of government that is supposed to represent the interests of the people? What if the Court used its legal powers to overwhelm the will of the people expressed in the elective branches? Hamilton tried to relieve these concerns, arguing "The judiciary, on the contrary (to the other two branches), has no influence over either the sword or the purse; no direction either of the strength or of the wealth of the society; and can take no active resolution whatever. It may truly be said to have neither FORCE nor WILL, but merely judgment; and must ultimately depend upon the aid of the executive arm even for the efficacy of its judgments." Hamilton asserted that of all the branches, the judicial branch would be least likely to become tyrannical.

Overall, then, the Federalists argued that a stronger national government would be needed to make the United States survive over many generations. At the same time, they claimed that the new Constitution would not work against the spirit of the Declaration of Independence. The new Constitution, they argued, would not create a new form of tyranny; rather it would protect Americans' liberties and create conditions for them to pursue happiness. The separation of powers system and federalism were the two most important constitutional principles that would prevent the new government from being a form of tyranny. Of course, the American Framers did not invent either of these ideas: federalism emerged organically from history, as the thirteen colonies with different pasts came together to fight a war of Independence. And the idea of the separation of powers can be traced back to ancient Rome. When James Madison penned the federalist papers, he was well schooled in European thought of the mid-eighteenth century. The Baron de Montesquieu had also elaborated the idea of a tripartite system which was composed of an executive, a legislative, and a judicial branch.

Separation of Powers and Federalism in Japan and the United States

Many Japanese have already studied and learned about the separation of powers in their elementary schools. But they do not learn that systems of separated powers are qualitatively different in countries across the world. It can be said that the American separation of powers system is more rigid than the Japanese one. As Federalist Paper No. 51 stressed, the main objective of the American Constitution was to prevent power from being concentrated in too few hands.

The parliamentary system of Japan is very different than the Presidential system in the United States in which the power of the chief executive, or Prime Minister, is distinct and separated from the legislative branch. To become Prime Minister of Japan, for example, Abe Shinzo had first to get elected in his Yamaguchi's House of Representatives 4th

District. Then he was elected as the head of the Liberal Democratic Party, by the members of the House. Because the LDP was the majority party in the House of Representatives, he was elected as the Prime Minister. Therefore, Prime Minister Abe is both a Diet member and the head of the executive branch.

By contrast, under the American presidential system the President is not a congressman. President Barack Obama was a Senator, but he quit that position when he was elected as the President. He was not allowed to have positions both in the legislative branch and the executive branch. Obama got elected in the nationwide election that was separate from the congressional elections.

Because of the differences in the electoral systems, the relationship between Abe and his party, the LDP, is much closer than is the one between Obama and his Democratic Party. Because Abe was elected by the LDP, theoretically the LDP is expected to agree with all the policies that Abe supports. On the other hand, Obama was not elected by his fellow Democratic Congressmen. The party leaders in Congress feel less of responsibility to support policies that Obama proposes. Conversely, Obama, though the leader of his political party, has less influence over the individual members of Congress.

The role of the judicial branch is also different in Japan and the United States. The U.S. Supreme Court has been criticized as an "imperial judiciary" because the decisions have had large social and political impacts. For better or worse, the U.S. Supreme Court has a larger presence in the separation of powers system than its Japanese counterpart.

After the separation of powers, the second constitutional principle which is supposed to prevent the national government from becoming too dominant is federalism. Because American federalism really makes the American political system so different from many other countries, Chapter 4 of this book is devoted to discussing it. For now, suffice it to say that in a federal system, the national government does not have the final say in many policy areas. Rather, it shares policy making with the states, and in some cases may not interfere with what the states are doing. Many Japanese people might confuse American federalism with a decentralized administration of policy, *chiho bunken*, which some reformers advocate. That idea is very different from how federalism works in the United States, and the degree of autonomy the states have in the American federal system goes beyond the imagination of many Japanese.

Each state, considered to be a counterpart of a prefecture in Japan, has its own constitution. It also had its own militia and police. As Chapter 1 describes, each state functioned more like a country under the Articles of Confederation. The formation of states preceded the formation of the United States. As a result, states have sovereign power over their territory, at least in several policy fields. With American federalism the states gave up some of their sovereign power to the national government. By contrast, the goal of Japanese decentralization is to diminish some of the power of the national government, and to try to make each prefecture more than just a branch office of the national government.

The Powers of Congress and the Bill of Rights

When the Constitution was debated, leaders from the states were especially concerned about how to limit the power of Congress, which all agreed would be the primary branch of government. One way to limit its power was to expressly state what powers it would have, and to then declare that all other powers would be reserved to the states. So, Article 1 Section 8 of the Constitution "enumerates" what the Congress can do. The first enumerated power is today called the "taxing and spending clause." It reads, "The Congress shall have Power to lay and collect Taxes, Duties, Imposts and Excises, to pay the Debts and provide for the common Defence and general Welfare of the United States; but all Duties, Imposts and Excises shall be uniform throughout the United States." After this broad power to lay and collect taxes are eighteen other expressed powers.

The idea of the enumerated powers is a guarantee that the national government would not multiply and expand its power over time. But many of the Anti-federalists still worried about this, in part because of ambiguity of the definitions. For example, there was no clear definition of "general Welfare of the United States." Although Article 1, Section 9 lists things the Congress cannot do, the Anti-federalists wanted to further secure the rights of Americans against the national government. They suggested that the Constitution include a list of rights that the American people possessed that the new government could not violate. George Mason, for example, was one of three delegates who attended the Convention but did not sign at the end because he wanted more explicit guarantees in the Constitution that state's rights and individual rights would be protected. So, he demanded a Bill of Rights – much like his home state of Virginia had, to protect the citizens of Virginia from the federal government.

Federalists rejected Mason's proposal at the Constitutional Convention. Later they agreed to include the Bill of Rights as the first ten

Date	Events	Vote (Y-N)
09/17/1787	Final draft of Constitution signed	
10/27/1787	First Federalist Papers published	
12/07/1787	Delaware ratified (1st state)	30-0
12/12/1787	Pennsylvania ratified (2nd)	46-23
12/18/1787	New Jersey ratified (3rd)	38-0
01/02/1788	Georgia ratified (4th)	26-0
01/09/1788	Connecticut ratified (5th)	128-40
02/06/1788	Massachusetts ratified (6th)	187-168
04/28/1788	Maryland ratified (7th)	66-11
05/23/1788	South Carolina ratified (8th)	149-73
06/21/1788	**New Hampshire ratified (9th)**	57-47
06/25/1788	Virginia ratified (10th)	89-79
07/26/1788	New York ratified (11th)	30-27
03/04/1789	New Congress began	
04/30/1789	G Washington became the President	
11/21/1789	North Carolina ratified (12th)	194-77
05/29/1790	Rhode Island ratified (13th)	34-32

Table 2: Timeline of the Constitutional Ratification

amendments *if* the state conventions would agree to ratify the constitution. Thus, the Federalists compromised with the Anti-Federalists because they thought that compromise would make the ratification process easier. Most Americans are very grateful for that compromise, and the Bill of Rights is one of the most celebrated parts of the Constitution today. Thanks to the compromise, in June 1788, New Hampshire became the ninth state to ratify and the Confederation Congress accepted the ratification of the new constitution (see Table 2).

As the Federalists promised, the first ten amendments – the Bill of Rights – were proposed immediately after the new Congress was in operation in 1789. The first amendment asserts that the national government should not infringe upon people's freedoms of religion, speech, assembly, and petition. The second amendment protects the right of people to bear weapons. The third through eighth amendments are all designed to protect American citizens from the coercive policing powers of government, and from being wrongly accused for crimes, or being punished too severely. The Supreme Court has drawn on this group of amendments to find a right to privacy that all Americans have. The ninth amendment asserted that the list of rights in the preceding amendments was incomplete, and that other rights not listed there should also be protected. Finally, the tenth amendment assures that the state governments have all the powers reserved to them that were not enumerated. It reads, "The powers not delegated to the United States by the Constitution, nor prohibited by it to the States, are reserved to the States respectively, or to the people."

The Amendment Process and Key Amendments since the Founding

The Framers understood that the Constitution would likely need changes in the future and wrote Article 5 to define the amendment process. The Articles of Confederation needed unanimous approval by all thirteen states to be amended. It was almost impossible to amend the Articles of Confederation under that rule. State constitutions, on the other hand, usually needed a simple majority of support from the people for amendment, and could be too easy to be changed. The new Constitution found a middle path between these two extremes that respected both the national and state governments. First, two-thirds of votes in each house of Congress could propose constitutional amendments. But, all amendment proposals then have to be ratified by three-fourths of the states before they have the force of law. Alternatively, upon a request by two-thirds of the state legislatures, Congress can call a national constitutional convention to amend the Constitution. But, this has never happened in American history.

It has been very difficult, though not impossible, to amend the Constitution. Since 1791 with the adoption of the first ten amendments as the Bill of Rights, the constitution has been amended only 17 times. Although some amendments address technical issues, such as pay for members of Congress, others had greater impact on the political system of the United States. The amendments include the eleventh (1798), which clarified the power of the judiciary; the twelfth amendment (1804), which clarified the process of electing the President and Vice-President; and the twentieth (1933), which clarified the dates for the terms of office of the President and Vice-President. The twenty-second was ratified in 1951 to prohibit Presidents from serving more than two four-year terms. The original Constitution did not stipulate how many terms a person could serve as President. However, George Washington declined an offer to run for a third term although he would have been almost surely reelected. He believed that the President should not stay in his office too long. This action became an informal norm for the following presidents. However, under the circumstances of the Great Depression and World War II, Franklin D. Roosevelt was elected for a third and then a fourth time. The twenty-second amendment made Washington's belief officially written into the Constitution.

The most significant amendments to the Constitution are those that reshaped American society and democracy. The thirteenth (1865), fourteenth (1868), and fifteenth (1870) amendments were ratified after the Civil War to abolish slavery in the United States and regulate the civil rights of

American blacks. The thirteenth amendment reads, "Neither slavery nor involuntary servitude, except as a punishment for crime whereof the party shall have been duly convicted, shall exist within the United States, or any place subject to their jurisdiction." The fourteenth amendment, discussed more fully in Chapter 4, asserted federal authority over the states, and prohibited the states from denying the "equal protection of the laws" to any persons living within their territory. The fifteenth amendment prohibited the states from denying voting rights to men because of their race or national origin. Together, these Civil War amendments were designed to incorporate blacks into the American republic, and they empowered the federal government over the state governments. However, the equal rights of blacks were not immediately enforced, and southern states wrote new electoral laws that made it very difficult for blacks to vote, including literacy tests and taxes on voting. Legal equality for blacks in the United States would not be secured until key Supreme Court cases and Acts of Congress almost a century later (see Chapter 4).

Several other amendments have greatly expanded American democracy. The seventeenth amendment (1913) changed elections for the US Senate; instead of being elected by the state legislatures, Senators would now be elected directly by a statewide popular vote. The nineteenth amendment (1920) declared that "the right of citizens of the United States to vote shall not be denied or abridged in the United States or by any state on account of sex." Before that amendment, women in a majority of states were not allowed to vote in national elections, although women in the Western states had secured voting rights as early as 1869 in Wyoming. The woman suffrage movement, which grew out of the abolitionist movements of the 1840s, began pressuring Congress to grant female suffrage in 1870, but it took a half a century for the movement to finally secure that right in 1920. Women's voting rights have shaped American elections and policy, and impacted the subsequent women's movements and the development of American social policy.

Finally, a small wave of amendments that were ratified toward the end of the Civil Rights movement of the 1960s and 1970s helped to expand American democracy further. The twenty-third amendment (1961) granted a right to vote in presidential elections to the citizens of Washington, DC. Today the residents of Washington, DC still do not have full national voting rights, and have no representatives in Congress. The twenty-fourth amendment (1964), made taxes on voting illegal and the twenty-sixth amendment (1971), extended voting rights to all citizens who were eighteen years or older.

Although the Constitution has been amended, it has survived without a full revision. Rather, the amendments have made the Constitution more legitimate by reflecting changing social and political demands. The U.S. Constitution is the oldest national constitution still in force in the world. Its longevity is due in part to the fact that it is a short and vague document. The vagueness has allowed it to be interpreted differently at times. But more importantly, Americans, consciously or unconsciously, think that the Constitution is a contract for them to be an American nation, a contract for states to form a country, and to form a more perfect Union.

Americans believe that their constitution makes the United States exceptional in the history of the world. In fact, it did create a more democratic political system than the world had ever seen. In the late eighteenth century, the United States was in the vanguard of democracy as it spread around the globe; particularly, it inspired the French Revolution. Thus, the Constitution is not only the history of the country but also a symbol of democracy worldwide. Americans are very proud of this political heritage.

Cross-Cultural Dialogue 2:
The Constitution in Japan and the United States

Michael : "Teaching the Introduction to American Politics course to my American students at Wake Forest University in North Carolina is a real pleasure, especially when we study the American constitution. Starting in kindergarten (at six years old), and more intensely in the fourth grade (at 10 years old) my students have already been schooled in the basics. Although very few are familiar with the detailed history and contents of the Constitution, knowledge of the Constitution is a must for all Americans. Is there a founding political document in Japan that has an equally powerful status? Do you think the Japanese would ever feel the same way about their current constitution as Americans feel about theirs? Why or why not?"

Taka : "The U.S. Constitution is a powerful document for Americans because it holds heterogeneous Americans together and creates a sense of American-ness. To the Japanese, written documents, including their Constitution, are less important. Japanese-ness is based largely on unwritten customs and even non-verbal com-

munications – in Japanese, *a-un no kokyu*. Moreover, the history of the current constitution matters. The Japanese Constitution was written during the U.S.-led military occupation after World War II by the strong leadership of General Douglass MacArthur. Some appreciate the Constitution because of its Article 9 for Pacifism, but others denounce it as the "MacArthur Constitution" and seek to write a new constitution. Probably, most Americans would be surprised to learn that the Japanese people have a debate on whether their constitution is truly their own constitution or not."

CHAPTER 3

Westward Expansion, Civil War and the Progressive Era
西部への膨張、南北戦争、革新主義時代

　建国期から約100年で、アメリカ合衆国は大西洋に移民した300万人の小さな国家から、一つの大陸を制し、太平洋の島々にまで膨張した帝国となった。西部や領土拡大では、奴隷所有を許可する州（奴隷州）と奴隷所有を禁じる州（自由州）との対立が深まっていった。この奴隷制をめぐる対立は南北戦争につながった。そして同じ対立構造は戦後再建にも影響を及ぼしたのである。また奴隷制はアメリカを分断しただけでなく、連邦政府の権力を限定的なものとし、州政府の権利を保持する役割を果たしたのである。そして南北戦争の戦後処理が終了した後、連邦政府の権利は拡大し始め、それと同時にアメリカが世界においてどのような役割を果たすべきかを模索する時代になった。

The First Vote, by Thomas Nast (1867). The drawing is optimistic that blacks will quickly become full citizens of the nation after the emancipation of the slaves and the end of the American Civil War. Courtesy of the U.S Library of Congress.

During the century after the Founding, the United States grew from a small nation of 3 million people settled on the Atlantic Coast, to a continental empire stretching all the way to islands in the Pacific Ocean. The expansion of the country to the West, and the incorporation of territories increased the conflict between the slaveholding and non-slaveholding states of the North and South. These tensions culminated in a Civil War over the issue of slavery, and decades of rebuilding the nation after the war. Slavery not only divided the United States but also limited the power of the federal government and secured the states' rights. After the Civil War, the federal government began to expand its power and reformers struggled to increase the rights of American citizens, reduce the amount of corruption in politics, and adjust to the reality of the United States' emergence as a world power on the global stage.

In 1790, the total population along the Atlantic Coast not including Native Americans was 3.9 million. Among the white population, 65 percent were English, five percent Scottish, and four percent German. Slaves of African descent formed 18 percent of the population, and the Southern economy rested on their forced labor. In just one state, South Carolina, 43 percent of the population was slaves, and they were a great source of wealth and power for the white families who owned them. Northern families also farmed. In addition, in large towns and the big cities of Boston, New York and Philadelphia, there were significant financial and manufacturing trades.

From these origins, the American nation changed dramatically over the nineteenth century. The different economic interests of the Northern commercial states and the Southern agricultural states whose prosperity depended on slavery, was the basis of a major sectional division within the nation. As the U.S. Congress acquired all of the continental territory spreading toward the Pacific Ocean (for the admission of new states, see Figure 3),

Americans in the North and South disagreed about the future of slavery in the new territories. This disagreement led to a Civil War (1861-1865) during which over half a million Americans lost their lives. Northerners dramatically changed the Constitution after the War, redefining who counted as American, enhancing the rights of American citizens and altering the relationship between the federal and state governments.

After "Reconstruction" of the Southern states, the United States continued its expansion into the Caribbean and the Pacific and began to engage fully with Asia for the first time. Domestically, economic disagreement between farmers, trade unions, factory workers; an emerging middle class in cities; and the immense power of national corporations led to a populist movement, and set the stage for the Progressive Era. By the first decades of the twentieth century, the federal government had expanded its power over national policy, and the U.S. was no longer isolated from Europe and the rest of the world.

No.	State	Year	No.	State	Year	No.	State	Year
1	Delaware	1787	18	Louisiana	1812	35	West Virginia	1863
2	Pennsylvania	1787	19	Indiana	1816	36	Nevada	1864
3	New Jersey	1787	20	Mississippi	1817	37	Nebraska	1867
4	Georgia	1788	21	Illinois	1818	38	Colorado	1876
5	Connecticut	1788	22	Alabama	1819	39	North Dakota	1889
6	Massachusetts	1788	23	Maine	1820	40	South Dakota	1889
7	Maryland	1788	24	Missouri	1821	41	Montana	1889
8	South Carolina	1788	25	Arkansas	1836	42	Washington	1889
9	N. Hampshire	1788	26	Michigan	1837	43	Idaho	1890
10	Virginia	1788	27	Florida	1845	44	Wyoming	1890
11	New York	1788	28	Texas	1845	45	Utah	1896
12	North Carolina	1789	29	Iowa	1846	46	Oklahoma	1907
13	Rhode Island	1790	30	Wisconsin	1848	47	New Mexico	1912
14	Vermont	1791	31	California	1850	48	Arizona	1912
15	Kentucky	1792	32	Minnesota	1858	49	Alaska	1959
16	Tennessee	1796	33	Oregon	1859	50	Hawaii	1959
17	Ohio	1803	34	Kansas	1861			

Figure 3: Admission of New States

The 1860s was a turning point for the United States. It was for Japan as well. Within two decades after contact with the United States in 1853, Japan was increasingly influenced by Western powers in its internal affairs. Displeased with that meddling, the lower samurai class along with a rising commercial middle class in Japan overthrew the Tokugawa Shogunate and reinstalled the Emperor as the head of state. From 1868, the Meiji government sought to expand the military, promote technology, introduce the new education system, strengthen the power of the central government, and expand Japan's influence in the Pacific. By 1900, Japan had won a war with the Chinese for control of the Korean peninsula, and in 1905 it stunned Europe and the United States when it defeated Russia on land and sea. Before the Meiji Era ended in 1912, Japan had become a major imperial power with colonies, and it had one of the most educated populations in the world.

Thus, the nineteenth century was a period of comparable transformational political change in Japan and the United States. In a rare coincidence of global history, the starting points for these changes occurred in nearly the same years. Despite the significant cultural, historical and linguistic divide that separated the two countries, a common trajectory emerged out of the 1868 Restoration in the case of Japan, and the 1868 Reconstruction in the United States. In both countries, an intense period of state building emerged, the energy for which was guided by fervent nationalist ideologies and an ethno-centric conviction that their distinctive "peoples" (much more homogenous in the case of Japan) had the right and the power to extend their influence across the globe, with Japan moving west toward the mainland of China, and the United States moving west toward Japan.

The Early Republic, the Rise of Sectionalism and Mass Democracy, 1790-1830

Americans from the North and South lived different lives that varied by culture, by educational and economic opportunity, by their economic systems, and by their ethnic and class diversity. They held stereotypes about what people from other sections (or regions) were like. For example, in 1780

Thomas Jefferson, the author of the Declaration of Independence and the third American President wrote: "Northerners are cool, sober, laborious, persevering, independent, jealous of their own liberties, superstitious, and hypocritical in their religion." Southerners, on the other hand, "are fiery, voluptuous, indolent, unsteady, independent, zealous of their own liberties but trampling on those of others, generous, candid and without attachment or pretensions to any religion but that of their own heart."

These descriptions exaggerate differences; nevertheless, they reveal that many early Americans viewed each other with suspicion. More significant than these stereotypes was the wide gulf in economic opportunity for young white Americans in the North and South. In Massachusetts, boys and girls benefitted from a tradition of basic education dating back to the first Puritan settlements of the 1630s. The family of a young boy whose father was a lawyer might have enough resources to send the boy to "Boston Latin," one of the oldest public grammar schools in the world. If the boy did well, he could then attend Harvard College, established in 1636, and now Harvard University. By contrast, in South Carolina, there were no public schools until after the Civil War ended in 1865. Unless a boy came from a wealthy slaveholding family, there was little opportunity to get a basic education or to pursue a professional career.

The economic systems of the North and the South had different foundations, but they were interdependent. The Northern economy rested on banking and finance, the manufacturing of arms, ships, textiles; the Southern economy focused on the agricultural production of tobacco and cotton. The two sections traded with each other across state lines and they traded on their own terms with foreign nations, especially England and France. The North's need for Southern cotton and other agricultural products tied the two economies together. In addition to trade, the memory of the American Revolution helped to forge common bonds between Northern and Southern Americans who otherwise lived distant lives from one another. Yet, as the country expanded its territory West, conflicting visions about the future mattered more than memory of the Revolution.

When George Washington left office in 1796, he asked the country to avoid the "baneful effects of the spirit of party." Giving advice that Democrats and Republicans might heed today, Washington argued that the spirit of party "serves always to distract the public councils and enfeeble the public administration. It agitates the community with ill-founded jealousies and false alarms, kindles the animosity of one part against another, and foments occasionally riot and insurrection." Despite his warnings, a heated presidential contest emerged between John Adams, the Vice President who favored a strong federal government, and Thomas Jefferson, the Secretary of State, who favored a weak federal government. Jefferson lost the election by 3 electoral college votes (see Chapter 6), but his supporters, the Democratic-Republicans mobilized to secure his victory four years later. Guided by the political ideals of Jefferson, the Democratic-Republicans controlled Congress and the Presidency for a generation, until the election of Andrew Jackson in 1828.

Despite Washington's early warnings about faction, the idea that the North and the South each had its own political identity and independent interests (sectionalism) became more and more prominent. During James Monroe's presidency (1813-1821), a major shift in political relations between North and South occurred with the Compromise of Missouri, an act of Congress carefully struck to maintain the balance of power in the nation between the free states of the North and the slave states of the South.

When Congress enabled territory to become the state of Missouri, Northern members of Congress refused to admit Missouri unless another state would be admitted as a free state – the state of Maine which was to be separated from Massachusetts. Recognizing the need to create a formula for the admission of new states in the future, Congress declared that any territory admitted above the longitude extending West from the southern border of Missouri would be free, and any below it would allow slavery. With this Act, Congress for the first time passed a law that legitimated slavery. To an emerging group of ardent activists in the North who wanted to abolish slavery outright (the abolitionists), the compromise was unacceptable.

Andrew Jackson's election to the presidency in 1828 marked several major shifts in American politics. Born in Tennessee, a relatively undeveloped "Western" state not one of the original 13 colonies, Jackson was a man of the people, and from a different social class than the six preceding Presidents who belonged to the elite. His election was not possible without the support of the first mass-based political party in the world – the Democratic Party. What the Party stands for has changed dramatically over American history, but it still exists today, led by President Barack Obama. The original Democrats, many of them white supremacists, never could have imagined that an African American man would lead the Party and sit in the White House.

During the 1820s, many states eliminated property as a qualification for voting. In the 1828 presidential election, tens of thousands of middle class and poor white men voted for the first time, and they supported Jackson against the incumbent John Quincy Adams. Jackson's campaign portrayed Adams as an elitist who did not understand the common man. Jackson's base in the new Democratic Party was in the South and the Western states, though small farmers, laborers and European immigrants throughout the country also supported the party. Jackson was an ardent supporter of the Union, on the one hand, but he also opposed a national banking system. Prior to the Civil War, the Democrats were opposed by the Whig Party, who generally favored a national bank, high tariffs, and "internal improvements" of the country's infrastructure. The Democratic-Whig party system lasted until the Civil War, when most Whig supporters became Republicans.

Slavery Divides the Nation, Civil War and Reconstruction, 1830-1880

In 1831, a Virginian slave named Nat Turner led a slave rebellion against their white masters, killing 60 white men, children and women.

Turner's goals were to terrorize the white slave-holding class, and to seek revenge for the human suffering slaves endured, which included being lashed, and having their family members be sold like property to other white owners living far away. Turner and 30 other rebel slaves were caught, tried and executed. In the same year, William Lloyd Garrison, a white lawyer from Massachusetts, published the first issue of the Liberator, an anti-slavery publication. Southerners condemned the paper, arguing that any black slaves who could read it would "learn" about the injustice of their condition, and be moved to rebellion.

The 1830s to 1840s is a radical period in American history. For the first time, activists throughout the country began a concerted campaign to free all slaves and to establish political and social equality for blacks. By 1840, abolitionists sent thousands of petitions to members of Congress, pressuring them to debate an end to slavery. John Quincy Adams, the only person to serve in Congress after being President, received the most of these letters, and he became famous for raising the issue again and again on the House floor, even after the leadership in the House passed a rule prohibiting discussion of the slavery issue.

The Capture of Nat Turner, by William Henry Shelton (circa 1840s). Source: www.learnnc.org.

The controversy over slavery intensified as the country expanded to the West. A great debate emerged over the annexation of Texas. Texas was a Mexican territory settled by white American settlers and slaves since 1820. After Texans declared independence from Mexico in 1836, many Texans wanted their territory to become one of the United States. Texas statehood and whether slavery would be permitted there became a major issue in the 1844 presidential election. When James Polk won the race, he supported admitting Texas as a slave state and Oregon as a free state, again to balance the power between the free states and slave states. Congress caused a war with Mexico and annexed Texas. As part of the terms of peace, Mexico ceded to the United States all of the land that now makes up California, Arizona, New Mexico and Colorado. Acquisition of the new land created tension because the nation had to decide which part of the land would be free, and which would permit slavery. This tension was temporarily reconciled in an Act of Congress, known as the Compromise of 1850.

Events between 1854 and 1860 culminated in a terrible Civil War that begin in 1861 and lasted until 1865. The war eventually claimed 625,000 lives – more than the total casualties of Americans in all wars the United States has fought since. Following one of the deals set in the Compromise of 1850, the Act of Congress admitting Kansas and Nebraska to statehood empowered the residents living there to vote on permitting slavery. Nebraskans voted in large numbers to prohibit slavery in their constitution, but in Kansas the outcome was unclear. Slaveholders and abolitionists flocked to the state to make it their own. Northerners believed that the law violated the rule laid down in the Missouri Compromise of 1820, which had banned slavery in territory north of the southern border of Missouri.

A coalition of people angry about the law formed the Republican Party. This included Free-Soilers, who argued that slavery degraded the dignity of white men's labor and who wanted cheap land for whites to own in the West; Northern Democrats, who were frustrated by the control Southern Democrats exercised over the Senate; and anti-slavery Whigs, who supported an increased role of the government in the economy, high tariffs and investments in transportation and education. For the next five years, pro-slavery and anti-slavery forces settled in Kansas, each group try-ing to maximize their numbers and thus secure an outcome in their favor. Battles with casualties occurred between these two groups of settlers, and the nation was shocked at the violence, which they called "Bleeding

Kansas."

John Fremont from California was the first Republican to seek the Presidency, but he lost by a significant margin to James Buchanan, a Democrat from Pennsylvania. Three days after Buchanan became President, the Supreme Court ruled infamously in the case *Dred Scott* v. *Sanford* (1857), that the "the Negro has no rights which the white man is bound to respect." In the case, a slave named Dred Scott sued his owner for his freedom after having spent time living with him in a state that prohibited slavery. The Court ruled that Scott, because he was a black man, had no rights to sue in court. The Court also ruled that the Missouri Compromise of 1820 was unconstitutional, and argued that Congress had no authority to make a uniform rule that defined which states could practice slavery. This case enflamed abolitionists and encouraged politicians, such as Abraham Lincoln, a state Senator from Illinois, to run for higher office. Originally, Lincoln only opposed the expansion of slavery into new states; he did not support freeing the slaves, or ending the slavery in the original colonies of the South.

In addition to Bleeding Kansas and the Dred Scott decision, the trial of John Brown was a final event that framed the election of 1860, which elevated Lincoln to the presidency, and which led to the secession of Southern states from the Union. Brown was a white man from Massachusetts who with his sons in 1856 murdered five pro-slavery whites. Then in 1859, he led an unsuccessful attempt to seize a federal battery of weapons in Harpers' Ferry, Virginia. He was charged with treason, and during his trial, he pleaded forcefully in religious language about the injustice of slavery, before being hanged. After Northern newspapers

Abraham Lincoln (1864). Photograph by Anthony Berger. Courtesy of the U.S. Library of Congress.

praised Brown as a martyr to a just cause, and after Lincoln was elected on a ticket opposing slavery in the West, the South realized that the North was firmly against them. Even though Lincoln had campaigned to allow slavery to continue where it already existed in the South, Southerners never forgot his famous statement in a speech in 1856 that "a House divided will not stand." Lincoln boldly asserted that "the nation cannot remain half free and half slave" and "that it must become all one thing or the other."

After the election, with Republicans in control of the Executive branch, a chain of Southern states seceded from the Union, starting with South Carolina, a state whose slave population had increased from 43% during the founding to 60% at the outset of the Civil War. This increase in the slave population was a huge increase in the wealth and property of the white plantation masters, which they were quite determined to protect. Eventually 10 states left and formed the Confederate States of America, with its capitol in Richmond, Virginia. Even at that point, Civil War was not inevitable. Conceivably, the United States government could have conceded the secession, and forged international relations with a new nation on the American continent. Lincoln, however, was firmly committed to the idea of keeping the Union together. In addition, Northerners wanted to keep the Union together in order to keep Southern agricultural production and commerce within the control of the United States. In fact, the Northern plan to emancipate all of the slaves did not emerge until the middle of the war. As the war continued, abolition became the guiding moral rationale that justified the terrible violence and bloodshed.

After the war ended in 1865, Congress and President Lincoln, and then President Andrew Johnson after Lincoln was assassinated, faced several problems. The most pressing was how and under what terms the Confederate States would be readmitted to the Union. The second pressing problem was how to incorporate the four million slaves freed by the war into Southern society and to the rest of the nation as free citizens. The

Reconstruction, by J.L Giles (1867). An image of post-Civil War reconciliation between the North and South, which shows lifting up a unified country with the American flag draped on top. Although North and South were reunited, racial discrimination remained in South. Courtesy of the U.S. Library of Congress.

third problem facing policymakers was how to rebuild the Southern economy without slave labor, and how to continue the production of cotton, essential to the textile industry of Northern cities, while also promoting industrialization in the South. During this period of Reconstruction, Congressional statutes, amendments to the United States constitution and bureaucratic policies administered by federal officials addressed these problems. Reconstruction lasted from the end of the War until 1877, when President Rutherford Hayes removed federal troops from the South. Quickly, the former slave-holding elite within the Democratic Party in the South regained control of the Southern state legislatures.

Congress required each of the former Confederate states to rewrite their constitutions before Congress would readmit them to the United States. Their new constitutions had to declare political, though not economic or social equality, for black and white citizens, and they had to demonstrate a commitment to public education for poor whites and the newly freed slaves.

The Southern Reconstruction constitutional conventions are fascinating. For example, the delegates to South Carolina's 1868 constitution who debated and wrote the new constitution included former slaves and their former masters. Congress also created and the federal executive administered a Freedman's Bureau to aid newly freed slaves on their path to freedom. The Bureau provided income assistance, food and general aid to help slaves become economically self-sufficient. The Bureau failed, however, and most former slaves become sharecroppers – tenants on white owned farms who had to give nearly all of what they produced to the white owners. These black sharecroppers accumulated massive debts to their white landowners. With large debts, they had little freedom to leave and to work in other jobs of their choice. In some states, such as Mississippi, white legislatures passed laws called the Black Codes, which criminalized blacks who tried to escape the sharecropping system.

Because of these Codes, and because Northern Congressmen in the Republican Party were skeptical that white Southern leaders would make sincere efforts to ameliorate the living conditions of blacks, Congress enacted several important amendments to the U.S. Constitution. The Southern states were required to ratify these amendments before they could rejoin the Union. The Thirteenth Amendment in 1865 made slavery illegal, the Fourteenth Amendment in 1868 declared that blacks were citizens, and the Fifteenth Amendment in 1870 declared that the right to vote could not be denied because of race (though, it could be denied because of sex).

In the South, the popular response by whites to these Amendments was negative. Most white Americans at the time believed in the superiority of the white race, and Southern whites did not appreciate Northern imposition of racial equality. Extreme white supremacists formed "societies" like the Ku Klux Klan (KKK), who used violence to terrify the black population. The goal of the KKK was to "save" white European civilization from miscegenation – the racial mixing of blood and culture through marriage and reproduction. Formal equality for blacks in the South was not a reality until the victories of the Civil Rights movement in the 1950s and 1960s (discussed in more detail in Chapter 4).

From Populism to Progressivism, 1880-1920

After the Civil War, a rapid industrial development took place in the United States. The success of the railroads and widespread technological innovations empowered many corporations to increase the scale of their operations. Confronted by a patchwork of federal, state and local laws, the directors of corporations such as Standard Oil – the world's first billion dollar corporation – saw a great advantage in pulling together all of the different parts of their business into one Trust. They used legal and illegal means to squeeze competitors out of the market. With their monopoly power, the owners of trusts like Standard Oil had the power to lower wages for workers, raise prices for their goods and to make extravagant donations to elected politicians in the state legislatures and Congress. The political system became terribly corrupted and it was often asserted that big corporations were more powerful than politicians in Washington, DC.

Populism and Progressivism were two great responses to the rise of corporate power. The Populist movement originated in the 1870s among small land-owning farmers in the South and the West. The farmers resented the control that large railroad companies had over prices for transporting agricultural products and high Tariffs on European goods. Among other things, the Populists asked for regulations of big corporations that would generate economic competition across state lines – and that would allow them to cooperate with labor unions (see Chapter 11).

Populists also supported changes to the monetary system. In 1896, William Jennings Bryan, a Senator from Nebraska became the Democratic Party nominee for president after he delivered his famous *Cross of Gold* speech. The speech railed against corporate greed. Bryan argued against the Republicans' view that economic prosperity could be secured by allowing individuals to amass large fortunes; rather government should ensure goods for the producing classes – the farmers and laborers. Bryan lost the Presidential election to William McKinley who successfully portrayed the Populists as too radical. Although the populist movement died out after that election, many of its causes, and especially the goal of reducing the economic and political power of big corporations, were carried on by the Progressives.

The Progressive Era from 1890 to 1920 in American history is named after the political reforms sought by middle class professionals who worried that industrialization, urbanization, and immigration seriously threatened the health of the American nation and corrupted the virtues of the American people, and thus weakened the stability of the Republic. Progressives challenged the increasing power of wealthy businessmen and the corruption of the two major political parties. They asked for federal regulation of monopolies, higher income taxes for the rich, child labor laws, a minimum wage for workers, the direct election of U.S. Senators by the people, popular primary elections in place of party elites selecting political candidates, the popular initiative and referendum, and women's suffrage.

"*The Awakening*" by Hy Meyer (1915). Women's suffrage spreads from the western states to the east.

A major goal of the Progressives was to restore virtuous American values. Therefore, their efforts also included social reform. They warned that American values were threatened by drunkenness, low quality education, and foreign cultural values. Moreover, they pushed for more restrictive immigration legislation and Americanization programs, a constitutional ban on alcohol, compulsory education laws, truancy officers, and increased funding for schools. Finally, their support for women's suffrage reflected their moralistic politics. Because women avoided partisan politics, many Progressives believed that women could "clean up" the

American political system, if only they had the right to vote. Once women finally secured the right to vote in 1920, many celebrated their new rights by going to the polls. Today, most political scientists agree that women's right to vote and their increasing presence in government has changed the policy priorities of lawmakers, who now pay more attention to women's social and economic situation.

Cross-Cultural Dialogue 3: Traveling Across the Nation

Michael : "I grew up in New Jersey, one of the original thirteen colonies on the Atlantic coast. I knew nothing about the Midwest or the West until I went to graduate school in Madison, Wisconsin and later traveled to Los Angeles, Seattle, and even to Hawaii. Now, I live in North Carolina, a former part of the Confederacy, where it's common to see statues honoring Confederate war heroes. All of this is to say that the United States is a HUGE place with a complex history! The distinct history of these places sometimes makes them feel like they are different countries – and yet, national obligations bind us all. These cultural differences confront Americans immediately when we travel across the country. I wonder, to what extent does traveling across Japan reveal to the Japanese a sense of cultural diversity rooted in the past of the different regions in Japan?"

Taka : "Michael, your questions remind me of the importance of the comparative study! This is a very interesting question. For me, Okinawa is a good case to consider. It used to be its own kingdom, the Ryukyu Kingdom, and had original culture and language. I grew up in Fukui which is close to Kyoto, the Japanese old capital. When I  went to other parts of Japan – Tokyo, Tohoku, Shikoku, and Kyushu, I felt that there are some cultural variations in those areas. But my visit to Okinawa was a very different experience. The Okinawa culture – including architecture, music, and also delicious Okinawan food! – gave me a feeling of being in a very different culture than the rest of Japan."

CHAPTER 4

Federalism, Civil Rights and Interstate Commerce
連邦制・公民権・州際通商

19世紀から20世紀にかけて、アメリカの連邦政府はその機能を劇的に発達させ、そして州政府に対する権力を拡大させた。特に人種政策と経済政策という二つの政策分野がこの変化を起こしたといえる。第一に、合衆国憲法修正第14条は州に対して法の下の平等を元奴隷であった者を含め何人にも否定してはならないとした。そして連邦政府はそれ以降特に南部州の人種的マイノリティーの権利を保護するためにその権力を拡大させた。第二に、19世紀末から連邦議会や大統領は、経済を安定成長させるために連邦政府の州際通商を規制する権限の必要性を主張するようになった。アメリカの連邦制―連邦政府と州政府との権力の均衡―はアメリカの政治史を特徴づけるものである。そしてそれが他の国と比べてアメリカの国内政策を独自のものにしているといえる。

Nettie Hunt sits on steps of the Supreme Court of the United States, holding a newspaper and explaining to her daughter the meaning of the decision, *Brown v. Board of Education* (1954), which held that segregated schooling systems in the American states violates the "equal protection" clause of the fourteenth amendment to the U.S. Constitution. Photo published in 1954 by the *New York World Telegram & News*. Courtesy of the U.S. Library of Congress.

Over the course of the nineteenth and twentieth centuries, the federal government of the United States dramatically increased its capacity and its power over the state governments. Two policy areas in particular shaped the course of these changes: civil rights and interstate commerce. First, the Fourteenth Amendment of the Constitution guaranteed that no state should deny their citizens the equal protection of the laws, and the federal government increased its power over time to protect the rights of racial minorities, especially in the Southern States. Second, starting at the end of the nineteenth century, Congress and the President leaned on the federal government's authority to regulate interstate commerce in order to manage the nation's economy. The shape of American federalism - the balance of power between the national and state governments - makes American political development distinct, and it continues to make domestic public policy in the United States unusual in comparison to most other countries around the globe.

Chapter 3 traced how westward expansion, the American Civil War and the Progressive era changed American national identity and American political development. The addition of new states in the West increased the geographic size of the nation, and contributed to tensions between the North and the South over the issue of slavery that ultimately led to a Civil War. A new nation was reconstructed out of the rubble and ashes of that war, and the most important political change was the increasing power of the federal government to intervene and alter laws and policies within the state governments. Although the period of Reconstruction after the Civil War was full of promise of guaranteeing to black Americans their civil rights, in fact those rights took almost a century to secure. Thus, the protection of civil rights led to an increase in federal power.

In addition, just as the Civil War made possible a long century of change in the area of civil rights, it also recreated the American economy on a national scale, as slave based agriculture was extinguished in the South, and railroads and other new forms of technology like the telegraph provided the infrastructure for a national economy and large national corporations to emerge. As those corporations and large banks controlled more and more of the economies of the several states, Progressives and the Democratic Party began to leverage the power of the federal government to regulate and limit the power of those national corporations. After the Great Depression, Americans came to see the federal government in a new light, as having the legitimate authority to intervene in the economy to benefit the general welfare of American citizens.

The development of American race relations and commerce across state lines, as with other public policies in the United States discussed later in this book, take their shape because of American federalism. In federal systems like the United States, different levels of government – national, state (prefectural) and local – bear responsibility for different areas of policy. By contrast, in unitary political systems, such as Japan, policymaking is centralized at the national level and is administered fairly uniformly throughout the rest of the country. In unitary systems, officials at different levels of government are less likely to have different prerogatives, and are less likely to clash. Instead, lower level officials are expected to carry out the agendas of the higher level officials in the national government. In federal systems, by contrast, we cannot assume this consensus. Rather, officials in the national, state and local governments try to protect their prerogatives on the one hand, while also trying to forge beneficial and cooperative relations with officials working at a different level of government, on the other. In the United States, understanding how federalism works is especially important for understanding domestic public policy. The federal government, by contrast, controls foreign policy. This chapter highlights how relations between the federal and state governments have changed over time.

How the United States Became a Federal System

As Chapter 2 discussed, what American federalism would look like was the main subject of the debate between Federalists and Anti-federalists during the state conventions to ratify the U.S. Constitution between 1787 and 1791. These debates occurred prior to the formation of most of the world's nation states. The Americans had fought a revolution against England, controlled by a monarch and parliament; the other countries of Europe also had imperial ambitions across the globe; and elsewhere in the world, most territory was ruled either by dynastic royal families, as in China, or by military rulers, as in Japan. The Americans viewed these other models of political organization as tyrannical. Yet, they also understood that a weak union of the thirteen colonies into a mere confederation of states would jeopardize Americans' position with respect to Europe. The debates in the ratifying conventions focused on just how strong the new central, federal government should be; and what powers – or policy areas – it would have primary authority in, and which powers and policy areas, by contrast, would be left to the states. These concerns are primarily laid out in Article 1 Section 8 of the Constitution, which enumerates the powers that Congress has, and the Tenth Amendment to the Constitution, which explicitly states that all powers not specifically assigned to Congress and the new federal government would be reserved to the people, or to the states.

It is important to note, however, that what the American federal system would practically emerge to be – just how expansive the powers of Congress would become; to what extent the relations between federal officials and state officials would be cooperative or antagonistic; and, what should be done constitutionally if those relations became antagonistic – is nowhere specified in the words of the Constitution. In fact, the terms, "federal" and "federalism" appear nowhere in the document. Rather, American federalism is a contested constitutional principle. In other words, what American federalism was, has been and will be is constantly being worked out practically as American officials at the national and state levels interact with one another to confront public problems and develop policy responses to those problems. Furthermore, as these practical relations are negotiated, and as conflicts between federal laws and state prerogatives fail to be reconciled, the Supreme Court of the United States has entered the politics of federal relations as a major player. Because tensions between national and state actors ultimately comes back to issues of constitutional interpretation, the Supreme Court has frequently had to step in as an "umpire" who decides what authority the federal government possesses, and what policy areas the states control, which the federal government may not encroach upon.

How Federalism Changed because of Civil Rights

Until the end of the Civil War, Americans were governed by two sovereign authorities: the state in which they lived and the federal government – this is known as dual sovereignty. Each of these levels of government was primarily responsible for different arenas of policy: the federal government was in charge of foreign policy, interstate commerce, and a national currency, and the state governments were in charge of all other policy areas: policing, health, education, welfare, roads and other infrastructural investments. When it came to these latter domestic policy areas, the citizens of different states really lived under different legal and policy regimes; foreign and economic policy, though, bound them together under a common national citizenship. However, all Americans, no matter where they lived, shared a political culture of needing to secure their rights against the government. In effect, dual sovereignty meant that the rights of Americans needed dual protection. While the Bill of Rights to the Constitution protected the rights of white men from the national government, it did not protect them against their state governments. Any protections the residents of the states enjoyed against their state governments were spelled out in state law: either in the state constitutions or in statutes enacted by the state legislatures.

A good example of how this dual system created inequalities in access to basic civil and political rights is the case of African Americans. Until the Civil War, African Americans were not legal persons unless state governments declared them to be so. African Americans might be citizens under the laws of a given state, but until after the Civil War, they were not citizens under the laws of the federal government. That is, none of the rights in the U.S. Constitution protected them at all. Furthermore, the federal judiciary

Dred Scott (1888). Painted by Louis Schultze. Courtesy of the Missouri Historical Society.

was not a venue through which they could seek protections either from the actions of the federal government, or from the white people in the states in which they lived. This is what Justice Taney meant in the infamous Supreme Court case, *Dred Scott* v. *Sandford* (1857) when he said, "The negro has no rights which the white man is bound to respect." After the Civil War, Congress and the states ratified the Fourteenth Amendment, which sounded a death knell for this claim. The Amendment's significance for American political development cannot be overstated. For the first time, the American constitution declared that all persons would be protected by the national Bill of Rights against any unjust laws passed by the state legislatures. The language is important:

All persons born or naturalized in the United States, and subject to the jurisdiction thereof, are citizens of the United States and of the State wherein they reside. No State shall make or enforce any law which shall abridge the privileges or immunities of citizens of the United States; nor shall any State deprive any person of life, liberty, or property, without due process of law; nor deny to any person within its jurisdiction the equal protection of the laws.

The purpose of the first sentence was to assert that all blacks are citizens, no matter what state they lived in. In addition, this clause also for the first time made it clear that all persons, regardless of race, and as citizens of the United States would be protected against any states that "make or enforce" laws that "abridge the privileges and immunities of citizens of the United States." Even more significantly, the Amendment created a new right for the residents of the states: that no state would "deny to any person within their jurisdiction the equal protection of the laws." The "equal protection clause" is so important. Most advances in promoting equality among racial, ethnic and religious groups in the United States are based on this clause.

Many Supreme Court cases have shaped the constitutional meaning of the equal protection clause, and shifted federalism as a result. Here, we focus on two that deal with race, and one that also addresses race, but more fundamentally addressed the voting rights of all Americans. Today, every American learns about *Plessy v. Ferguson* (1895), which established that the federal government could do very little to alter race relations in the South, and the landmark case, *Brown v. Board of Education* (1954), which over-turned the ruling in *Plessy*. *Brown* determined that racial segregation in the United States was not constitutional. While in *Plessy*, the Court set a precedent of deferring to state and local policies that established separate public accommodations for whites and blacks – an example of national power deferring to states' rights, in *Brown*, the Court established that national power would be asserted to ensure equal access for all races to public accommodations.

The details of the two cases and the Court's reasoning in each case are interesting and important. Plessy was an African American resident of New Orleans who violated a city policy by boarding an all-white trolley train. When the conductor asked him to get off, he refused and was arrest-ed by the police. Plessy sued the city, arguing that banning him from the trolley because he was black denied him equal protection of the law. The Supreme Court ruled against him, holding that so long as the city operated a separate system of trolleys for blacks, then the city was not violating his equal right to access public accommodations. In the famous words of the court, "separate but equal" facilities, segregated by race did not violate the Fourteenth Amendment. That interpretation of the equal protection clause ruled constitutional law for more than half a century, and it permitted states to pass racially discriminating laws, so long as any publicly provided goods were at least made available to both races. Thus, if a state offered public education to whites, it was also required to offer public education to blacks, but the ruling meant that segregated schooling systems would be permitted.

Brown v. Board of Education (1954), overturned that rule. The Browns, an African American family living in Topeka, Kansas, sued the city's school board for not allowing their children to attend the all-white schools. The Browns argued that even though all black schools were open and available to their children, the schools were hardly equal in quality. Even more important, the Court argued that inequality in terms of resources and the quality of teaching, etc. was not the main injustice. Even if there were equality of resources, segregated schools should still be considered unconstitutional because the existence of the segregated system itself cast a shadow of inferiority on black children. The very fact of the segregated system – that blacks and whites should be separated and should not live together, marked blacks as an inferior class. The Supreme Court in Brown agreed with these arguments,

Nine black students were escorted by federal troops to attend a white high school (1957). Because Central High School in Little Rock, Arkansas and the Governor of Arkansas refused to let them attend the school, President Eisenhower sent the federal troops to achieve the racial integration guaranteed by the Board of Education decision. Courtesy of Central High Museum Historical Collections/UALR Archives.

and declared that the segregated schooling systems of the Southern states were unconstitutional. This was a tremendously important decision. With it, the federal government clearly asserted its authority over "states' rights" to legislate in a policy domain not expressly given to the federal government by the Constitution. The Southern states refused to comply with the ruling, rendering the power and the authority of the Court suspect. But, within a decade, because of the willingness of the President in the executive branch to require Southern school districts to admit black children, and because Congress eventually threatened to withdraw federal funds for education in the South if the Southern districts did not comply, the Southern schooling systems were significantly integrated by race.

A few years after the *Brown* case, *Reynolds v. Sims* (1962) addressed the voting rights of citizens and fundamentally changed the patterns of American politics. In *Reynolds*, voters in Alabama sued state officials for failing to reapportion districts for the state legislature after the 1960 census. Alabama was composed of 67 counties, whose people were represented by 106 representatives and 35 Senators. The state constitution required that each county have at least one representative, regardless of how many people lived in it; and that the state would be divided up into 35 Senate districts, with each district having one Senator, and no county being represented by more than one Senator. The voters sued because the legislative districts had not been changed since 1901, despite the fact that there had been significant population changes across the counties, and there were large inequalities in population across the counties. The result was that many of the state's legislators represented vastly unequal numbers of people. In the extreme, one Senator represented 40 times as many people as another. Voters argued this violated the Fourteenth Amendment, since the district system meant that the some citizens had forty times the voice and influence over their representatives than other citizens. The Supreme Court agreed with these arguments and ordered state officials in Alabama to redraw the district scheme so that all representative and senatorial districts represented roughly the same numbers of people. This case is important for federalism because it made clear that the federal government had sovereign authority to determine what state representative schemes looked like – a clear statement of federal authority over states' rights.

How the Federal Role Has Increased because of the Powers of Congress

The previous section examined how federalism changed over time in the domain of civil rights. In this section, we examine shifts in federalism because of the power that Congress wields, enumerated in the Constitution. Many of the legitimate increases in the power of the federal government to shape policymaking in the states are traceable to Article 1, Section 8 of the Constitution. Most opposition to this increasing power of the federal government is based on different interpretations of this clause and on the Tenth Amendment, which explicitly states that any powers not expressed are reserved to the states and the people. The fact is that the federal government is now far larger than the Founders anticipated it would become.

The important role that Section 8 has played in expanding federal power was envisioned by critics of the Constitution during the ratification debates. One anti-federalist from New York who wrote under the pseudonym, Brutus, worried about three clauses in particular: first, that "Congress shall have the Power to lay and collect Taxes ... to provide for the common Defense and to promote for the general Welfare;" second that Congress has the power to "regulate Commerce ... among the several States," known today as the interstate commerce clause; and third, that Congress will have the power "to make all Laws which shall be necessary and proper for carrying into Execution" the enumerated powers. Controversy endures because the Constitution was designed to make the federal government more powerful than the national government had been under the Article of Confederation, *and* to place limits on the federal government.

The most significant developments have turned on controversy over the power of Congress to "regulate commerce." As with changes in federalism because of civil rights, many Supreme Court cases deal with the commerce issue. Here we mention only four cases. First, in *Gibbons v. Ogden* (1824), Ogden sued for his right to operate boats traveling between the two states of New Jersey and New York after state officials in New York granted a New York boat company a monopoly on navigation in the Hudson River. The Supreme Court had to decide whether commerce only meant the exchange of goods or in addition, if it meant the navigation of goods to be bought and sold. In a plain ruling, the Court ruled in Ogden's favor, arguing that any activity going across state lines could be regulated by Congress – but business occurring within state lines could not. Because navigation was commerce across states, Congress had clear authority to regulate it.

Second, the meaning of the commerce clause was rearticulated more than a century later in another highly influential case, *Wickard v. Filburn* (1942). In that case, the U.S. Department of Agriculture had a policy limiting how many acres farmers could farm in order to stabilize the prices of agricultural goods. When a farmer named Filburn farmed more acres of land than the U.S. Department of Agriculture had permitted, he was penalized, and then he sued. He argued that growing wheat to feed his own farm animals was not "commerce." The Supreme Court disagreed, asserting that Congress's power to regulate commerce extended to local production and consumption of goods, if the added effects of local actors had substantial effects on commerce across, including prices, state lines. This interpreta-

President Franklin Roosevelt's administration created unprecedented regulations of agriculture (1936). Courtesy of the National Library of Agriculture.

tion significantly increased the federal role in regulating the economy within state boundaries.

In contrast to these two expansive rulings, two more recent cases illustrate how the Supreme Court will also limit expanding the regulatory power of the federal government. In *U.S. v. Lopez* (1995), the Supreme Court struck down a law enacted by Congress that prohibited the sale and purchase of guns near schools. The U.S. government penalized a man named Lopez for selling guns near a school in violation of the law. He appealed, and argued against the U.S. government that local gun sales could not be regulated by Congress, since the "point of sale" of the gun occurred within a local jurisdiction only, and not across state lines. The Court agreed with Lopez.

Finally, and most recently, in *National Federation of Independent Business v. Sebelius* (2012), the Supreme Court upheld the key component of President Obama's signature domestic policy achievement: the Patient Protection and Affordable Care Act to expand health care coverage to millions of Americans. Among other things, the law requires all Americans to have health insurance – whether through their employer, from a government program, or purchased on their own in health care exchanges. The most controversial provision was an individual mandate which imposes a penalty for those who do not have health insurance. The Court disagreed with the Obama administration's argument that the penalty was justified under the commerce clause, but upheld the penalty as a legitimate use of Congress's power to tax. Some legal scholars argue that the Supreme Court's ruling is a legal precedent which will limit in the future how federal actors can use the commerce clause to justify federal regulation of economic activity in the states.

Federalism as Cooperation between Governments

The federal government and state governments do not always fight over which level of government should deal with public problems. In fact, federal and state officials work together to administer many programs, such as Medicaid, which provides health care for the poor. As was discussed above, from the Founding until the Civil War, the dominant idea of federalism was that of dual sovereignty: the federal government and state governments were sovereign in distinct policy fields, and that sovereignty structured a dual form of citizenship. But as the federal government expanded its role in economic and social policy after the Great Depression, a more cooperative relationship between the federal and state government emerged. "Cooperative federalism" refers to positive and constructive relationships between federal and state actors from these periods.

However, as the role of the federal government increased, federal officials began to intervene more in states' jurisdictions. Some scholars call this top-down relationship, "regulated federalism." Then in the late 1960s, the Republican President, Richard Nixon introduced policies that restrict the power of the federal government – a shift that scholars call the "new federalism." This shift occurred in response to declining public support for the policy programs of the New Deal and Great Society coalitions led by Democratic Presidents (see Chapters 11 and 12). The 1980 election of Ronald Reagan advanced the conservative agenda to scale back the scope of federal power. In the 1980s, conservatives promoted devolution of policy-making from the federal government down to the states – including in the administration of programs like Medicaid. To do this, they replaced categorical grants to the states, through which state officials received federal dollars to implement policies developed by the federal government, with block grants, which also gave federal dollars to state governments, but gave state officials more discretion in how they would use the money. Using money to shape policymaking in the states in this way is referred to as "fiscal federalism."

As the Court case reviewing Obama's health care law reveals, fiscal federalism is itself contested. How the federal government uses its great fiscal resources to get the states to do things may be less cooperative than it is coercive. Certainly, cooperative fiscal federalism is welcomed in the states in many policy areas – a good example is in support of building roads. On the other hand, many state officials also resist fiscal federalism in other policy areas – such as in health care and education. In fact, in the case of *National Federation of Independent Bisiness v. Sebelius*, the Supreme Court struck down the federal government's ability to withdraw all funding from the existing Medicaid program if the states do not agree to expand coverage of the program to include more people. Although state officials tend to welcome financial support to aid their disadvantaged citizens, state budgets can become too dependent upon that financial support, and Congress and the President sometimes use that dependency to move states in certain policy directions. Some call that kind of federal manipulation of state prerogatives, "coercive federalism," and it often generates resentments. These dynamics will not disappear. Rather, they appear to be settling as an enduring feature of federal relations in the American political system.

Cross-Cultural Dialogue 4: What about Prefectural Rights?

Michael : "Americans have really mixed feelings about the power of the federal government. For example, when I was growing up in New Jersey attending the public schools there, my teachers taught me about how the federal government was good because it helped to secure the civil rights of American racial minorities. But later, when I was a graduate student I began to learn how teachers have come to see federal power in a more complicated way: while they would love to see money from the federal government to support their schools, they reject any attempt by federal officials to regulate the curriculum in their schools or to measure how well teachers are performing. All of this to say that on some issues, such as civil rights and funding, Americans desire more federal involvement in policy at the state level, while in others, such as curriculum development in the schools, they really oppose federal power. I've always wondered how Japanese citizens and politicians view the power of the national government of Japan, and whether they support taking decision-making power away from the national government and giving more of it to the Prefectural or city governments."

Taka : "Public school teachers in Japan actually have the similar attitude toward the central government, but for different reasons. Some Japanese teachers oppose the central government's intervention in deciding the contents of history textbooks and forcing teachers and students to sing the national anthem and hoist the national  flag. That's because they think that their historical memory, particularly about World War II, is different from the central government's. But other than that, Japanese people in general believe that the central government should be responsible for public education. American people refer to 'governments' at the state and local levels, but we do not usually use the word 'government,' *seifu* in Japanese, to refer to Prefectures and municipalities. While there have been calls for the decentralization of the political system, strong voices interestingly have come from the central government. But now Osaka city mayor Hashimoto Toru and others advocate the delegation of the central government' authorities to prefectures and municipalities. But I think it should be more difficult for Japanese people to imagine the decentralization than American people who have a strong tradition of states' rights."

CHAPTER 5

Social and Political Diversity
社会的、政治的多様性

　日本と比較すると、アメリカは人種的にも民族的にも多様性に富む国である。この多様性にはさまざまな起源がある。イギリスの植民地支配や奴隷制の遺産、建国後早い時期におけるヨーロッパ北部や西部からの移民、先住民部族、メキシコ領、カリブ海や太平洋の島々の征服、第二次世界大戦前までに来た新しい移民、そして1965年以降にラテン・アメリカ、アジア、アフリカ諸国から来た移民などが多様性を形成している。アメリカに来れば経済的な機会に恵まれるという希望を胸に多くの人々がアメリカに移住する一方で、宗教の自由も移民を引きつける一つの要因となってきた。さまざまな移民の歴史があったことで、アメリカで活気に満ちた経済や宗教の多様性が生まれたといえる。特筆すべきは、経済的利益をめぐる対立に加え、この膨大な社会的多様性が民主党と共和党というわずか2つの政党によって表出されているということである。両党の下に集まる連合は時代によって変化する。アメリカの選挙、政治文化、そして政策の方針をめぐる対立を理解するためには、アメリカ社会の社会的多様性についての基本的な知識を持たなければならない。

New York - Welcome to the land of freedom - An ocean steamer passing the Statue of Liberty: Scene on the steerage deck, with German Immigrants (1887). Courtesy of the U.S. Library of Congress.

Compared to Japan, the United States is a country of much more racial and ethnic diversity. This diversity has several roots: British colonialism and the legacy of slavery; the early immigration of Northern and Western Europeans; the American conquest of Native-American tribes, Mexican lands and islands in the Caribbean and the Pacific; and later immigration from Southern Europe prior to World War II, and from Latin America, Asian and African countries since 1965. While the promise of economic opportunity has always attracted people to the United States, so has the promise of religious freedom. The vibrant American economy and religious diversity in the United States stem from this rich history of immigration. Remarkably, the vast social diversity, in addition to conflicts over economic interests, is channeled through only two major political parties – the Democrats and Republicans. These coalitions have changed significantly over time. In order to understand American elections, political culture and conflict over policy visions, one must have a basic knowledge of the social and political diversity in American society.

Written into the great seal of the United States and on most American currency is the phrase, e *pluribus unum*: out of many, one. The phrase originally referred to Union of the thirteen colonies, but it now means an aspiration among many Americans to become one common people, a single nation forged out of racial, ethnic and religious diversity. Generally speaking, Americans do share a common ideology based on a liberal defense of individual rights, and an ambivalent impulse to limit the size of the federal government on the one hand, while also using government to promote equality of opportunity on the other hand. Despite this common core of beliefs, the two major political parties are very polarized, even as both claim to be the true champions of these ideals.

Ethnic Diversity

Diversity has confounded American national unity since the Founding. Colonial Americans had pushed Native Americans violently westward from the Atlantic Coast. African slaves were a large percentage of the population in the Southern states. Non-English European groups – especially, Germans but also smaller numbers of Irish, Scottish, Dutch and Swedish – had large settlements in the colonies, and French and Spanish settlers occupied much of the territory west of the Appalachian Mountains. The fact is that not all of the first Americans were white, Protestant Englishman. Nevertheless, to this day, a majority of Americans insist that the English language should be the official language of the country, and many believe that being Christian is an important part of American national identity.

The first major wave of immigration came over the turn of the twentieth century: in 1910, 13.7% of the national population was foreign born – the highest percentage in American history. Between World War I and the end of the Civil Rights movement, immigration continued, but at slower rates, and the percentage of American residents who were foreign born did not approach the 1910 high until about a century later. Not surprisingly, immigration is the primary source of American social diversity. In the last four decades, the percentage of Americans who have white/European ancestry has declined as immigrants from Central and South America and from Asian countries has increased (Table 5.1).

This rich history of immigration has created what social scientists call a multicultural society. Although individual hard work and educational opportunity makes social mobility possible for the members of all social groups, race and ethnicity continue to structure social status and individual life chances in the United States. Even today after the success of the Civil Rights movement which promoted racial equality, white, English-speaking, Christian Americans enjoy an informal "privileged" position in American society. These privileges have gradually faded over the course of American

	1850	1880	1920	1970	2010
Total Population (millions)	23.19	50.17	105.71	203.21	308.75
Foreign Born (millions)	2.25	6.68	13.92	9.62	39.96
Foreign Born (% of total)	9.68	13.32	13.17	4.73	12.94
	Racial Composition of Total Population (percentages)				
White	84.31	86.54	89.70	87.65	72.41
Non-white	15.69	13.46	10.30	12.35	27.59
Black	15.69	13.12	9.90	11.09	12.61
Hispanic, any race	N/A	N/A	N/A	4.46	16.35
Asian, Pacific Islander	N/A	.21	.17	.75	4.93
	Origins of Foreign Born (percentages)				
Europe, Canada	99.82	98.20	98.51	90.79	14.08
Africa, Caribbean	0.18	0.21	0.53	2.64	4.57
Central and South America	N/A	N/A	N/A	18.74	45.48
Asia, Pacific Islands	N/A	1.59	0.01	6.23	28.24

Source: US Census Bureau.

Table 5.1: Immigration to the United States, 1850-2010

history, but a legacy remains from laws and private policies that specifically advantaged white European groups over other groups.

Today, responses to national tragedies typify the complexity of social difference in a diverse country like the United States. In the summer of 2012 in Oak Creek, Wisconsin, a 40 year old white man opened fire in a Sikh *gurdwara*, a temple or house of worship. He killed the religious leader and five others, and injured a police officer before taking his own life. The response of the media to this event reveals how race, ethnicity and religion structure American public opinion. Media elites and political leaders immediately condemned the massacre as a tragedy. But, they framed it as primarily a tragedy for the Sikh community, rather than as an act of violence that affects all Americans. Sadly, the occurrence was not random or totally unpredictable. Instead, it was the outgrowth of the once strong, and happily dying off, American "tradition" of white supremacy. The killer belonged to an openly white supremacist rock band called End Apathy. His band sang songs about how American whites need to take "their" country back from non-whites and non-Christians – that is, from people with a "foreign look" and foreign language and foreign culture. Fortunately, moments of racial and ethnic violence like these are now rare. The vast majority of Americans understand that the United States is a country of immigrants, and that racial and cultural diversity is a positive byproduct of that fact.

Historically, the most significant racial divide lies between European Americans (whites) and African Americans descended from slaves and white Americans (blacks). From the founding of the nation to the Civil War, the American economy depended on the violent

The "First Family" - President Barack Obama, his wife Michelle, and their two children in the White House (2011). Source: www.whitehouse.gov.

exploitation of enslaved black Americans. Even after the Civil War, state laws and certain federal policies permitted discrimination against blacks, and formal political equality for blacks was not secured until the Civil Rights Act of 1965. Americans are familiar with this history and with the struggle for racial equality between whites and blacks. Most Americans agree that the election of Barack Obama to be President was a pivotal moment in American racial history. Notably, Obama is not the typical African American: in fact, his mother is a white woman from Kansas and his father was not American at all, but Kenyan. In American racial terms, however, the fact that one parent is black means that Obama is black. Obama's wife, Michelle, is a more typical African-American: she descends from American slaves. Americans of her great-grandparents' generation, let alone of her parent's generation, would not be able to imagine a "black" President or First Lady of the United States.

Of course, the black-white racial difference is not the only one that has a history, nor is it the only one that structures American politics today.

Having Mexican or Central-American ancestry is an important racial distinction in the American Southwest, and it has increasing importance in national politics. On the West Coast and in Hawaii, Americans of East Asian ancestry, especially from China, Japan, South Korea and Vietnam have also been subjected to racial discrimination. An increasing number of immigrants from the Middle East and South Asia have settled communities in the Midwest. Large numbers of South Asian Indians live in American cities, and the largest Arab population in the United States lives in Dearborn, Michigan. This racial diversity is reflected in the numbers in Table 5.1 above.

Religious Diversity

The United States is one of the most religious countries in the world because of immigration and the American political value of protecting religious liberty. Religious values shape public policy in the United States to a far greater extent than in Europe and many Asian countries, which have become increasingly secular over time. In this respect, the U.S. is more like other countries in the Western Hemisphere and countries in the Middle East. A 2017 survey by Gallup, a prominent American public polling agency, showed that 87 percent of Americans say they believe in God. A 2015 survey from the Pew Forum on Religion and Public Life found that 70.6% of Americans identify as Christian: 50.1% identify as Protestant and 20.8% as Catholic. Although Protestantism has had a great influence on American political culture, it is important to note that American Protestants are not a uniform group, and to note that the number of Protestants has been declining. In fact, according to the Pew Research Center, "the United States is on the verge of becoming a minority Protestant

"Washington at Prayer" painted by Charles Currier (circa 1850). Courtesy of the U.S. Library of Congress.

nation." In 2012, for the first time in American history, the presidential ticket of a major political party did not include a Protestant – Mitt Romney is Mormon and Paul Ryan is Catholic.

But Protestants remain the largest religious group. American Protestant churches participate in three different traditions: Evangelical (25.4% of Americans in 2015), Mainline (14.7%) and Historically Black churches (6.5%). Evangelical Christians, including the Southern Baptist, Pentecostal, Assemblies of God and Church of Christ denominations, are among the most active Americans in politics. Evangelicals place salvation through Jesus Christ at the center of their private *and* public lives. In contrast, the members of the older "Mainline" churches, including the Methodist, Presbyterian and Episcopalian denominations tend to believe that there are non-Christian paths to salvation. In addition, they tend to separate their private religious beliefs from public life.

Like Evangelicals, religion also shapes the political views of Catholics, though they are more politically diverse than Evangelicals. The number of Catholics has remained constant over the last several decades, but the non-white population has been increasing in American Catholicism. In 2019, 63% of American Catholics are white, 32% are Hispanic or Latino. In addition to these large Christian groups, and in addition to the 23% of Americans who do not affiliate with any religion, 1% is Jewish, 1% is Muslim 1% is Buddhist, and 0.5% is Hindu. The vitality of American religious life is attributed to the First Amendment of the Constitution, which keeps the government out of religions, and protects the liberty of Americans to practice any faith of their choice, or no faith at all. Increasingly, religious values have become a dividing line for political partisanship. How often a person attends religious meetings is an excellent predictor of which political party they will support, with higher levels of church attendance correlated with support for the Republican Party.

Economic Diversity

The United States is a country with extremely wealthy families, a large middle class, and 46 million people living in poverty (as defined by income). Incomes for American families have decreased and inequality in wealth between the richest and poorest Americans has increased since the 1970s. Economists and political scientists point to several factors that account for these changes.

First, the global economy and the American position within it drastically changed in the 1970s. Since the 1970s, other national economies have competed with and outpaced American production in manufacturing. For example, Japanese automobile manufacturing began to outperform American firms, reducing the blue-collar jobs in the United States. Second, a global oil crisis in the late 1970s hurt the American economy and American consumers, hitting hardest the middle class. Third, in a globalizing economy, the American firms looked for ways to use cheaper labor from developing countries. For example, Dell, a computer company, has created customer centers in India. This outsourcing of labor also means fewer

"The popular tendency to rail at wealth is not entirely justified," by Puck (1897).
Courtesy of the U.S. Library of Congress.

jobs in the United States.

Fourth, aligning with these changes in the global economy and the negative effects on American income equality were changes in American family patterns: divorce and the number of single parent households headed by women have dramatically increased since the 1970s. This increase correlates with rising levels of inequality because single parent households tend to have less income than married households, especially when the single parent is a mother who has to balance caring for children with a job – usually by working fewer hours a week – and whose job is probably lower paying than jobs in lines of work that men tend to go into.

Finally, American inequality has grown because of conservative retrenchment against government programs that Democrats and Republicans created together after World War II to bolster the middle class. Ronald Reagan won election to the presidency in 1980 on a campaign of more limited government and smaller taxes – themes that are still very powerful in American politics today, and which were echoed loudly in the 2012 presidential campaign. The retrenchment policy called for strong individual responsibility, but many poor people are not able to find well-paid jobs to make a decent living.

Political Ideologies

American children typically begin their school day by reciting the Pledge of Allegiance: "I pledge allegiance to the Flag, of the United States of America, and to the Republic for which it stands, one nation, under God, indivisible, with liberty and justice for all." The ideals stated in the pledge, and a Supreme Court ruling from 1942 which protects the right of children to refuse to say it for any reason, captures a tension in American politics between individual liberty and national citizenship. Americans certainly value loyalty and patriotism to their country. But, they also strongly celebrate individualism, and the right to "liberty and the pursuit of happiness," even if it sometimes comes into conflict with the national interest. This tension between national identity and community on one hand, and individual liberty on the other, is a key dynamic in American political history.

Polling agencies such as Gallup and the Pew Research Center regularly survey Americans about their political ideology – their ideas about the proper role of government in the economy and society. The main ideological cleavage lies between liberals and conservatives, with many Americans falling in between as moderates whose positions don't fully align with either the liberal or conservative ends of the spectrum. This ideological diversity is important because voting behavior and the policy priorities of officials in government follow from them, and the policy agendas can have a differential impact on America's different social groups. Because of these effects, the political ideologies people hold tend to correlate with their racial and ethnic identity, religious beliefs, and economic position in society. And of course, political ideology tends to correlate highly with partisan affiliation or partisan leaning.

Today, liberals (who also call themselves progressives) and conservatives continue to disagree about the extent to which the government should interfere in markets and local institutions to promote equality of opportunity. In a way, the ideal of equality of opportunity reconciles the promise in the Pledge of Allegiance of "liberty and justice for all." While all Americans claim to love liberty and equality, progressives and conservatives disagree about what "justice for all" should look like. There are two basic dimensions to consider. First are ideas about the proper role of government in the economy and in providing for the general welfare. Second are ideas about the proper role of government in promoting traditional values and permitting individual expression.

On the first dimension, progressives support government intervention in the economy and a moderate government redistribution of wealth to ensure a basic standard of living for all Americans. By contrast, conservatives prefer minimal government interference in the economy and they are opposed to government spending on social support programs. On the second dimension, progressives generally oppose government support for the traditional values of the majority white culture, especially Christian religious values, and they support a stronger role for government in protecting individual life-styles that counter those values. By contrast, conservatives support laws and policies that support traditional Christian values, and that limit forms of personal expression and behavior that go against those values. For example, on this second dimension, progressives tend to support and conservatives tend to oppose abortion rights and gay marriage.

Although liberals or progressives and conservatives disagree on many things, most Americans do share an abiding commitment to one highly importantly idea, which they have used to combat blatant forms of inequality: equality of opportunity. The truth is that Americans have become vastly more egalitarian over time in their support for using government to end discrimination against specific social groups, and to ensure a baseline of educational, economic and political opportunity for all individuals, regardless of race, ethnicity, religion and sex. Even politicians accused of discriminating against other groups will say their position is consistent with ensuring equal opportunity for all law-abiding citizens of the United States. However, while a broad consensus exists about the value of equality of opportunity, Americans disagree significantly over what policies they should adopt to ensure it. The political ideologies people hold definitely correlate with which political party they tend to vote for, especially in national elections, but how ideologies have aligned with partisan identities has changed significantly over the course of American history.

Political Parties

Remarkably, all of American social diversity is channeled into political action through only two major political parties: the Democrats and the Republicans, two of the oldest political parties in the world. Both parties are "big tents" – a circus metaphor that suggests that the coalition of social groups making up each Party is often strange. In national elections, liberals tend to vote for Democrats, while conservatives tend to vote for Republicans. In elections for state level offices, especially in the South, the correlation between ideology and party is less tight, and Southerners some-times cast votes for Republican presidential candidates while also voting for Democrats for state Governor or state legislator. The websites of the national party organizations – the Democratic National Committee (www.democrats.org) and the Republican National Committee (www.gop.com) – present what the parties stand for, and they suggest the coalitions who make them up. While there has been continuity in what they stand for, the coalitions in the electorate who support them and the policies the party in government pursues have changed considerably over time.

First, consider some of the continuities. Since Andrew Jackson's pres-idency (discussed in Chapter 3), Democrats have always claimed to repre-sent the "common man" and the "working class" against the interests of big businesses, especially financial institutions. They have always been more welcoming of immigrants, and more tolerant of social diversity and individ-ual expression, and less inclined to adopt a moralistic agenda than Republicans have been. As a result, Democrats tend to do very well in urban areas. By contrast, since the Civil War, Republicans have always been the party of capitalism, from their origins as the party supporting "free labor" and opposing slavery in the Western states, to their continued support for commercial interests and financial institutions. Republicans have been more suspicious than Democrats of the moral values and religious dif-ferences that immigrant groups bring with them, and they are more inclined than Democrats to support Americanization programs that assimi-late new social groups into their version of American culture and values.

However, these general continuities in partisan identity over time are much less visible than the stark changes in what each Party has stood for over time. The changes emerged as the partisan hatreds caused by the Civil War receded in memory; as new ethnic and racial coalitions support-ing the parties changed because of immigration and wars fought abroad; because of the Civil Rights movement from the 1940s to the 1970s; and finally because of the movement of religious conservatives toward the

Republicans, and religious and secular liberals toward the Democrats since the 1970s. The starkest change has been the regional support for each Party in presidential elections. Because the Republican Party was remembered for several decades in the South as the party of "northern aggression," the Southern states were firmly Democratic from the end of the Civil War until the 1950s – for almost one hundred years. However, Harry Truman, John F. Kennedy and Lyndon Johnson altered the regional partisan alignment by appealing to the increasing numbers of African Americans who had moved to find work in Northern cities, and by promoting civil rights policies for American racial and ethnic minorities. By the 1970s, the Democratic Party, not the Republican Party, which had waged war to end slavery, had clearly become the party of Civil Rights, and had alienated white Southern voters from their ranks. The result was a transformational party realignment: now, the Republican Party has its greatest strength in the Southern states, whereas the Democratic Party has its greatest strength in the Northeast and the West Coast. Tracking these shifts in regional support for the national parties are shifts in the social groups who support the parties and shifts in policy positions. Table 5.2 demonstrates the social groups and interest groups that tend to support Democrats and Republicans in elections, as well as the major stances of the national parties on key policy areas.

As Table 5.2 shows, the two parties are highly polarized on almost every issue – except for foreign policy and trade, where there tends to be more agreement. Democrats are more likely to support policies that benefit historically marginalized groups, including racial minorities and women, and non-religious Americans. By contrast, Republicans tend to be more conservative and support policies that maintain the privileges of the upper middle class and the wealthy, many of who but not all, are whites. A major base of support for the Republican Party are Evangelical Protestants and conservative Catholics, who believe that many important institutions including the media, the schools and the universities are controlled by liberals with secu-

	Democrats	Republicans
Social groups	White liberals, racial and ethnic minorities, urban residents	White conservatives, Evangelical Christians, suburban and rural residents
Interest Groups	Environmentalists, feminists, labor unions, civil rights organizations	Gun rights lobby, small businesses, energy companies, pro-life (anti-abortion) groups
Policy Positions		
Taxes	Progressive taxes, higher rates on the wealthy and corporations.	Flat taxes, higher tax burden on the poor and middle class.
Welfare	More generous benefits for unemployed and the poor.	Less generous benefits for the unemployed and the poor.
Health Care	Supports President Obama's health care law.	Wants to repeal President Obama's health care law.
Foreign Policy	In retrospect, opposes Iraq War; more supportive of UN; favors free trade, but also protective of American labor.	In retrospect, apologetic about Iraq War; opposes any deference to the UN; favors free trade, and permissive of businesses investing abroad.
Education	Supports teachers' unions.	Opposes teachers' unions; supports public funding for private schools.
Immigration	Opposes state laws that empower police to arrest people suspected of being here illegally; supports the DREAM Act, which would allow children of undocumented immigrants to become citizens.	Supports state laws that empower local police to arrest people suspected of being immigrants; opposes "pathways to citizenship."
Women's issues	Increased public funding for child care; support abortion rights; affirmative action hiring policies that benefit women; and equal pay for equal work legislation.	Opposed public funding for child care; pro-life agenda; opposes affirmative action and equal pay legislation.
Civil rights	Opposes voter ID laws, supports affirmative action policies, and laws to reduce segregation.	Supports voter ID laws and opposes affirmative action policies; and opposes laws that would reduce segregation.
Energy	Supports alternative, non-fossil fuel based energies like wind and solar; opposes nuclear energy.	Less supportive of alternative energy sources and more supportive of nuclear energy.
Environment	In favor of strong regulations of business to protect American water and air.	Opposes environmental regulations that interfere with economic growth.
Transportation	Supports more investment in public transportation.	Less supportive of investments in public transportation.

Table 5.2: Party Coalitions and Policy Positions

lar values who oppose traditional morality. Another major difference between the parties is their geographic support: almost every rural area where whites live tends to lean Republican, whereas almost every single major city in the United States leans strongly toward the Democrats. Finally, the Democrats tend to support policies that redistribute money and wealth through the tax code to bolster the middle and lower classes, including public funding for health care, unemployment, retirement, and education at all levels. Unfortunately, political ideologies and partisan identities have become tighter over the years, which leads very frequently to partisan gridlock in the federal government as officials in government from different parties find very little to agree upon, and find it very difficult to compromise on their principles to work together. This clash of ideologies and the partisan conflict is one reason why the national debt in the United States has grown dramatically in last decade, and why many analysts are worried the leaders of the parties will be unable to reach a balanced approach to raising revenues (taxes) and cutting spending.

Cross-Cultural Dialogue 5:
Cultural Divides within Japan and the United States

Michael : "One of my best friends from college is from Montana, a very rural state. He bought a handgun as soon as he was 18 years old – the legal age for owning a gun. Almost every young man in Montana buys a gun when he comes of age – it's part of a culture of open spaces where hunting is a common sport. That culture is so unfamiliar to people who live in urban areas. In big cities, there are also many guns, but people in cities associate them with violence and illegal drugs, not with sports and recreation. Gun rights activists are mostly from rural areas and gun control activists are mostly from urban areas. These people see guns in totally different ways because of where they live. That cultural divide plays out in partisan politics, where Democrats and Republicans fail to see eye to eye on a sensible policy pleasing to both sides. When violence breaks out, like an elementary school in Connecticut in December 2012, when a young man used guns to murder 20 children only six years old, and several adults, gun control eventually bubbles up as an issue, but no one can agree on the right thing to do. Are there any issues like this in Japan, where people from different parties just cannot see eye to eye?"

Taka : "The debate about the Japan Self-Defense Forces (SDF) could be a similar case. When I ask my students if there are some values that hold Japan together, like the ideas of liberty, equality, and democracy for the United States, some students always say that pacifism is the fundamental value for Japan. They claim that Article 9 of the Constitution provides the core value that Japan has followed since World War II. In this view, pacifism makes Japan a unique country in the

world and the SDF should be used only for the self-defense purpose. But there is a different school of thought. Right-wing conservatives tend to think that Japan should become a 'normal country' and that the SDF should be recognized as the military and used for purposes other than self-defense, such as international peace keeping and other activities. It is very hard for the two groups to make a compromise. After hearing your story about the gun control issue, I think that the usage of violence, although of different kinds, divides the people both in Japan and the United States".

CHAPTER 6

Electoral System and Representation
選挙制度と代議制

　アメリカ合衆国は世界で最も古い代議制民主主義に根ざした国の一つである。代議制民主主義をアメリカが採用したのは日本よりも約100年以上前である。しかし、アメリカは普通投票権を確立するまでに法的にも実質的にも多くの障害があった。連邦政府でどのように人々の意思が表出されているかは建国期の遺産が影響している。それは独立した州の緩やかな連合体であり、君主制の否定であり、そして民主主義の行き過ぎへのエリートの恐れであった。また、第3章と第4章で述べたように、現在のアメリカの代議制民主主義の形は革新主義時代や公民権運動の遺産でもあるといえる。この時代に行われた改革によって、選挙権は女性や人種的マイノリティに拡大し、州レベルの選挙区が代表する人民の数を同数にし、連邦上院議員の選出法を直接投票とし、そして政党の候補者を決定するための予備選挙を導入した。この章では、アメリカの選挙制度の基本的な仕組みについて述べる。

President Joe Biden, 46th President of the United States.
Source: www.whitehouse.gov.

The United States is one of the oldest, representative democracies in the world. The nation adopted representative democracy about 100 years before Japan did, but there were many obstacles to universal suffrage during American history. The way the American people are represented in their national government is a legacy of the founding of the country, which was based on a loose confederation of independent states, a rejection of monarchy and on elite fears of excessive democracy. Representation in government is also a legacy of the Progressive Era and the Civil Rights movements, discussed in Chapters 3 and 4. Reforms during these periods extended the franchise to women and to racial minorities; required that electoral districts at the state level represent the same number of people; and undermined the power of political party elites. This chapter describes the basics of the American electoral system.

The President of the United States, the United States Senate, and the United States House of Representatives represent the American people in different ways. To understand these differences, first it is important to recognize that membership in Congress is organized geographically, and elections of members depend on social group differences and partisanship. Second, when it comes to making law, discussed in the next chapter, we must recognize that the Senate and the House aggregate interests in different ways – a majority in one chamber will be composed of a different coalition of interests than a majority in the other chamber. Furthermore, whereas majorities can easily pass bills in the House, minorities in the Senate can quite easily block legislation. Understanding each of these elements – who members of Congress represent, how they are elected and how elected officials vote to pass laws – is fundamental for understanding American politics. Finally, it is important to underscore that the President of the United States is the only official elected nationwide. The President is supposed to reflect the national popular will; the Senate is supposed to aggregate the interests of a majority of the states, regardless of their population; and the House is supposed to aggregate the interests of a numerical majority of the American people.

Who Senators and Members of the House Represent

While Senators represent entire states, members of the House represent specific congressional districts within each state. Unlike the House of Councilors and the House of Representatives in Japan, neither the American Senate nor the American House of Representatives adopts proportional representation. Members have to win in their own districts. The number of districts each state has depends on the number of people living in the state. The total number of offices in the House has been fixed since 1911 at 435, which means that the number of congressional districts each state has will change according to changes in its population, as those are measured every ten years by the federal government's census. After the last census taken in 2010, most states maintained the number of districts they already had, but several states gained districts while others lost them. For example, Texas, which has seen large population increases due to immigration from Central America, gained four new seats in the U.S. House. By contrast, Ohio lost two seats. Generally, the American population is moving from the Northeast and Midwestern states to the South and Western States. For example, consider changes since World War II: since 1945, California's seats have increased from 23 to 53, while New York's seats have decreased from 45 to 27. The number of seats each state has ranges from one in the six least populated states, to 53 in California – by far the largest state with a population larger than Canada. Figure 6 shows how the percentage of seats in Congress from each region of the United States has changed over time, from 1900 to 2010.

The federal government controls apportionment – the process that determines how many seats each state has – and the process is relatively automatic and it generates little controversy. After the census and apportionment, however, the state legislatures or special commissions in states

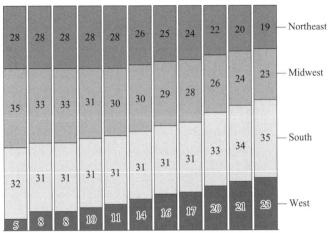

1900 1910 1920 1930 1940 1950 1960 1970 1980 1990 2000
Source: www.nationalatlas.gov.

Figure 6: Regional representation in the U.S. House of Representatives, 1900-2000.

with more than one representative have to redraw congressional district lines to reflect population movements within the state, and to ensure that each district has roughly the same population – around 720,000 people. This redistricting process is almost always controversial, as the political party in control of the state legislature after the census has the power to draw the district lines in such a way that will maximize the number of seats its party will control in the U.S. House. Political scientists refer to this practice of drawing politically advantageous boundary lines as gerrymandering.

Obviously, redrawing district lines does not apply to Senate districts, which are unchanged as long as the boundaries of the states are unchanged. The only time new Senate districts come into being is with the admission of new territories to statehood. The last two states to be admitted were Alaska and Hawaii in 1958 and 1959, which changed the composition of the Senate from 96 members to 100. Since then, the Senate has remained unchanged. However, as Chapter 3 illustrated, representation in the Senate was a highly contentious issue and the composition of the Senate and the balance of power between the political parties within it altered continually during the course of the nineteenth century as the country expanded westward. In the near future, the country is unlikely to admit any new states although a majority of the people of Puerto Rico, a Commonwealth of the United States, voted in the 2020 referendum to consider statehood. In addition, there is continual debate about Washington, D.C., a territory of the federal government, whose citizens lack representation in Congress, although they can vote for President. The fact that D.C. residents have no representatives in the House, and no Senators in the Senate strikes many Americans as unfair, especially Democrats, since most residents of D.C. identify with the Democratic Party. In fact, fewer people live in Wyoming than live in D.C., and yet the citizens of Wyoming have two Senators and one member in the House of Representatives. Debates over giving representation to the people living in Washington, D.C. are enduring.

Who the President Represents

Unlike in Japan, and in parliamentary systems generally, where the Prime Minister is first elected by the people of a legislative district, and then by the majority party coalition in the national legislature, in the American presidential system, the President's office is separate from Congress, and so is the President's election. All American citizens over the age of 18 may cast a vote for President (whereas the age is 20 in Japan). However an institution called the Electoral College, which is really more of a process and not a building where people work, determines who will be President. The framers of the Constitution designed the Electoral College to insulate the election of the nation's executive from popular majorities. Many Americans do not understand how it works. Probably the institution should be abolished, but the criticisms of it are overstated.

Here is it how it works. On presidential election days which occur every four years on the first Tuesday of November (the last one was on November 3, 2020), an American citizen goes to his local polling place, often a school gymnasium or a church meeting room, to cast a vote for President, Vice-President, members of the House of Representatives (who are elected every two years), and possibly one member of the Senate representing his state (who are elected every six years). In addition to national offices, he or she will probably be voting for several state offices (Governor, state legislators and judges), and also local offices such as for city council or school board, or county commissioner. For each office, *except*

Signboards in front of a polling place in Maryland for the 2012 election. A Romney/Ryan sign for the Presidential race is in the foreground. The "Vote for 6" refers to a referendum put to voters to decide whether gay marriage should by legal in the state of Maryland (discussed in Chapter 10). Photo taken by Takakazu Yamagishi.

the President and Vice President, his vote is fully counted as one vote, and it is tallied in the final vote counts. Whichever candidate gets the most votes for these offices wins – in most states, just a plurality and not a majority of votes is needed. His or her votes for President and Vice President, however, are mediated by the Electoral College.

The Electoral College is just the name given to the process that translates citizen votes into a final count – the Electoral College Count – that determines who will be president. This process has two stages: first each state translates the popular vote cast by the citizens into the Electoral College vote for that state; then all of the Electoral College votes from each state are added up, and which ever candidate has a majority of those votes becomes President. The number of Electoral College votes each state gets is determined by adding the number of Representatives the state has in the U.S. House to its number of Senators, which for every state is 2. So, Wyoming, with a population of around 580,000 people gets 3 Electors (1 House member plus 2 Senators), while California with a population of around 40 million people has 55 Electors (53 House members plus 2 Senators). For Presidential elections, then, we say that a candidate needs 270 Electors to win – one more than half the total number of Electors of 538

– reflecting 100 Senators, 435 Representatives, and 3 other Electors representing Washington, D.C.

When elections roll around, each major political party submits a list of Electoral College members to the state's elections board. These electors are real people – usually elites in the political party, such as the mayors of cities or towns. So, the Wyoming Republican Party would submit of list of 3 prominent Republicans in the state and the Democratic Party would submit a list of 3 prominent Democrats in the State. When a citizen of a state casts his or her vote for President, what they are actually doing is casting a vote to instruct the electors from the candidate's party to vote for the candidate he chooses. For example, when a Californian cast a vote to reelect President Biden in 2020, he was really voting to instruct the 55 Democratic Party electors to cast a vote for Biden. By contrast, a Californian casting a vote for Donald Trump was really voting to instruct the 55 Republican Party electors to cast a vote for Romney.

Conceivably, if the popular vote in a state splits 60% for Biden and 40% for Trump, then the Electoral College vote could also be split to reflect that, with 60% of the state's electors going for Obama and 40% going for Romney. But, that is not how it is done. Instead, all state legislatures except two, have decided that whichever candidate wins the plurality of the popular vote in the state, gets all of the state's Electoral College Votes. So, if 60% of the vote in California is for Biden, then Biden would get 100% of the state's Electoral College votes. Once the states translate their popular votes into Electoral College votes in this way, the total number of Electoral College votes is tallied up across the nation and whoever gets 270 or more wins.

However, because of the process by which popular votes are translated into Electoral College votes, it is possible that the winner of the popular votes (that is, whoever wins a plurality of all votes cast across the 50 states and Washington, D.C.), will be different from the winner of the Electoral College vote. This happened in 2016, when the Democratic candidate,

Hillary Clinton, won the popular national vote by about 3 million votes (65,853,514 to 62,984,828), but lost the Electoral College vote by 77 votes. Her opponent, Trump, won the Electoral College vote 304 votes to 227 and became President of the United States. The fact is that whoever wins the Presidency will claim to represent the entire American people. In fact, most Presidents govern as moderate leaders of their political party, always conscious of pleasing Independent voters – those who do not identify strongly with one of the major political parties.

Voters

Compared to elections for local office in the United States when it is common for less than a majority of eligible voters to turnout, in national elections, especially in presidential election years, turnout is relatively high at around 64%. The turnout rate of midterm elections (congressional elections without presidential election) however is much lower; sometimes as low as 30%. This rate is lower than rates in other countries in which voting is compulsory. It is often lower than other countries, including Japan, in which voting is not compulsory.

Two major factors lead to relatively low turnout: the sense among voters that their votes will not make much difference, either because they feel that the two major parties do not represent their interests or because there is little chance the candidate they support will win; and, voter registration laws that make it difficult for eligible voters to cast votes on election days. While every citizen over the age of 18 is eligible to vote, each citizen must actively register to vote before casting a vote. In some states, citizens are required to register 30 days or more in advance of the election. Since many citizens do not start paying attention to elections until a few weeks before they occur, it is not unusual for citizens who might have voted to be barred from voting because they did not register in time. Early voting laws, though, have made it possible for more people to vote before Election Day. In 2008, 31% of voters cast early votes, and the number was much higher, 65%, in 2020 due to the COVID-19 pandemic.

In the 2012 presidential election, controversy emerged over new voter photo identification laws which were passed by many state legislatures in 2011, in states controlled by the Republican Party. These laws require voters to present a government issued photo ID, such as a driver's license, at the polling place. States without such laws permit citizens to vote by checking the names and addresses of voters on voter lists, and having the voters sign their names. Democrats and many independents argue that such laws will have the effect of disenfranchising many young people, ethnic minorities and senior citizens who tend to be less likely to have the kinds of IDs required by the laws. In the summer of 2012, President Barack Obama's Department of Justice sued state officials for enacting these laws, arguing along these lines. In some cases, such as in Texas, the state law was overturned. The political buttle regarding ID requirements continued. After the 2020 election, Georgia put new restrictions and caused criticism by Democrats.

Primary and General Elections

Since the Progressive Era, voters, rather than political party elites have secured more influence in selecting their party's candidates who run in the general election against candidates from the other party. In the United States, party affiliation and membership for voters is very loose, and the requirements for membership are very minimal. Membership in a party is free – members do not have to pay any dues to the political party – and it takes no time commitment – the party does not require individual voters to actually do any work in the party. To become the member of a party, all a person needs to do is to officially declare their partisan affiliation with the elections board when they register to vote. Even at that point, voters need not declare any party affiliation. Most states, however, require that declaration before you can vote in a political party's primary election – the election that selects candidates to run in the general election against the other party. That is called a "closed primary" system. Yet, other states have "open primary" systems in which voters can vote in any primary election, regardless of their party affiliation. Thus, in every American state, and for every national office – Senate, House and President – elections occur in a two-stage process, and candidates for office actually have to wage two election campaigns.

In primary elections, candidates run to secure the nomination of their party in the electorate. The political parties in each state run their own primary elections, and these typically occur in the early winter or the spring. Whichever candidate wins the primary then has the Summer and early Fall to campaign for the Fall general election, which happens the first Tuesday in November, every two years for seats in the House, every six years for Senate seats (with a third of all Senate seats in play every two years), and every four years for the Presidency.

Incumbent Senators, Representatives and Presidents running for reelection might be challenged by candidates from their parties in primary elections. Such challenges are very rare, however, because challengers know it is extremely difficult to unseat an incumbent office holder. So, for a given seat, if there is for example a Republican incumbent, he will typically run uncontested in the spring primary. By contrast, there will be a strongly contested primary election to select the Democratic candidate who will challenge the Republican incumbent in the fall.

During the 2020 Presidential Election, primary elections began in February with Iowa, and ran until the end of June with Utah. For the presidential contest, the primaries select Delegates to the national Party conventions that occur at the end of the summer, where the delegates formally cast votes for the Party's nominee. President Trump ran uncontested in all of those primary elections. The Democrats by contrast had a highly contested primary season during the spring, until it was clear that Joe Biden, the former Vice president, had secured enough delegates to win a majority of votes at the national convention. For Senate and House primary elections, the voters directly vote for specific candidates. With the primary elections completed and nominees for the major parties selected, the nominees then began campaigning for the general election, which occurs in November.

For Presidential and many Senate elections, a noticeable shift in strategy occurs for candidates who won their primary elections against members of their own party, and who now must try to win a majority of the votes in their states, including votes cast by Independents and voters of the opposing party. This is an important difference: while candidates in the primary election appeal to the extreme ideological positions of voters in the electorate of their own party, in the general election, they must appeal to the center and ideological position of the median voter of their state. Thus the primary candidate tends to take more extreme positions – either more liberal if a Democrat or more conservative if a Republican – than he or she will take during the general election, when he or she will begin to speak more moderately. These shifts in tone and speech often lead general election candidates to contradict what they said during the primary season. If serious enough, the contradictions can become an electoral liability for the candidate.

For candidates (incumbents or challengers) for House seats, there is little shift in ideological positioning from the primary to the general election. Because most Congressional districts for the House are drawn by state officials in such a way that a large majority of the voters in the district are either Democrats of Republicans, Congressional district races are relatively safe, and whichever party controls the seat can safely push the party line without worrying about alienating Independents and voters from the other party. In these safe districts, which are about 90% of the 435 districts, incumbents nearly always win. In the remaining competitive districts, by contrast, where there is a roughly equal number of Democrats and Republican in the electorate, the ideological shift from the primary to general election common in Presidential and Senate campaigns is noticeable.

The strength of incumbents in the House and many Senate races results from other factors. They have a huge advantage over challengers because they are able to point to a record of achievements; because their prominent position makes it easier for them to command a lot of media coverage; and because most interest groups are more likely to give financial campaign contributions to those already in office, who have already proven their ability to win an election, than to a challenger who may or may not prove to have what it takes to win an election. Presidential elections and Senate elections, however, can be highly contested and reveal an American electorate that is extremely polarized. To limit the discussion here, we will focus on presidential elections.

Presidential Election Campaigns

Presidential elections campaigns are long, and candidates for office, whether the incumbent or potential challengers begin their campaigns a year and half to two years in advance of Election Day in November. During the 2020, election, Republican politicians hoping to run against President Donald Trump began announcing their campaigns in the spring of 2019, testing the electoral waters through polling to see if there was an interest in their candidacy. By the fall of 2019, there were more than ten serious contenders for the Democratic nomination, who engaged one another in nationally televised debates, and who sought constant media attention to enhance their name recognition.

In the 2019-2020 primary season, the televised debates led up to the early primary contests in February 2012 in Iowa, New Hampshire, Nevada, and South Carolina. In order to compete seriously, the candidates had to prove to the media that they could raise a lot of money from Democratic donors and liberal activists and they had to perform well in media interviews and on the debate stage. Because the candidates are all from the same political party and mostly agree in their policy positions, they try to outdo one another with clever statements that are either funny or controversial, and they try to turn the minor distinctions in their positions into large contrasts in ideology. Finally, each campaign makes a decision as to how positive or negative their attacks on opponents will be, especially in campaign advertisements on television, the internet and the radio, paid for by the campaign. Positive ads focus on the candidate's accomplishments and positive character traits; negative ads focus on opponents' failures, and criticize the character of opponents. To run a successful campaign, candidates also need to meet voters in town-hall meetings and on the campaign trail, shaking as many hands as possible. They need devoted followers who organize voters to vote for them in the primary elections.

And, yes, candidates need money to win the primary and general elections. They need to attract money from businesses, wealthy individuals, average voters and interest groups so that they can pay for campaign advertisements and "field offices" where activists work hard to "get out the vote" for their candidate. Of course, if the candidate is independently wealthy, as many of them are, they can use their own wealth to help fund their campaigns. In the 2019-2020, primary election cycle, there was no clear the frontrunner for the Democratic nomination in the early stages. By mid-Mach, however, Joe Biden, a former vice presidents, had secured the nomination, though formally, he would not become the nominee until the Party's convention in mid-August 2020. During the primary elections, President Donald Trump had little to do except to raise money, and to get ready for the general election campaign which would start only after it was clear who the Democratic challenger would be. Fundraising is critical for the presidential candidates not only for buying TV, radio and internet ads but also for opening local offices and hiring campaign staffs to make the election campaign more effective.

Who wins the Presidency during general elections is determined by the state of the economy; the ability of the political parties to mobilize their most devoted supporters (their base); the ability of the presidential campaigns to win over Independent voters, which means they must control the message about their campaigns as reported by the media; the personal popularity of the candidates; the performance of candidates during the presidential debates; factors beyond their control such as global economic recessions, and even the weather; and the campaign's financial war chest. To be successful, each candidate must raise as much money as possible to pay for campaign advertisements. Presidential elections are usually very nasty, with each campaign using more negative attack ads than positive ads. The negative ads sometimes include false information about the opponent, and almost always include misleading spin about the opponent's record. But political scientists have generally found negative ads to be both accurate and effective in reducing support for the candidate being attacked. For this reason, the campaigns use and will continue to use them.

Going into the 2020 presidential election, public opinion polls showed American voters divided in their support for President Trump and vice President Biden. In the final months of the campaign, all of the battles were fought in key swing states, or battleground states – states where there are roughly equal numbers of Republicans and Democrats , and the final vote in the state is very hard to predict. These states included Florida, Michigan, Pennsylvania, and Wisconsin. Most of the campaign money spent on advertisements and on organizing to get out the vote was spent in these states. Overall, the Biden campaign's primary message was that President Trump had failed to respond to the COVID-19 pandemic. The Trump campaign's primary message was that Biden could not be trusted to support polices that would benefit the working class. Both campaigns spent far more resources attacking their opponents than promoting their own accomplishments. In the end, Vice President Biden, won 51.3% of 155.8 million votes cast, and 56.9% of the 538 Electoral College votes.

Cross-Cultural Dialogue 6:
Electoral Controversies in Japan and the United States

Michael : "The 2000 presidential election was a painful and embarrassing moment for many Americans who take pride in their democracy. Al Gore, who won the popular vote by half a million votes, did not become president. When he lost the popular vote in Florida by only 547 votes out of nearly six million cast, he requested a recount of votes. The recount began, but controversy emerged as it became difficult in many cases to figure out which candidate a voter had in fact voted for. Eventually, the Supreme Court of the United States ruled in *Bush v. Gore* (2000) that the state of Florida must stop the recount. Not stopping it, the Court argued would be unfair to the voters living in other states, whose votes were not being verified. With that ruling, the Supreme Court – composed of non-elected officials – basically handed the Presidency to Bush. Gore, the statesman that he is, conceded the loss, but his supporters in the Democratic Party were furious. Since that election, there have been very negative feelings between the political parties, and the country has been very polarized in presidential elections, with neither side really trusting the other. I've always wondered about the perception of this debacle in other countries. Are there any comparable problems with elections in Japan? I would assume not!"

Taka : "I don't think many Japanese people can share your feeling that the 2000 election was a 'debacle of American democracy.' As we covered in the chapter, the Japanese Prime Minister is not elected by a nation-wide election. Moreover, especially under the long rule of the Liberal Democratic Party after 1955, the Prime Ministers were often decided by behind closed door deals among faction leaders. Many

Japanese don't know about or even don't care about how the process to select the Prime Ministers works, feeling that to choose the Prime Ministers is not their business. Furthermore, I think Japan and the United States differ not only in their electoral system but also in their image of leaders. When my son went to public school in the United States, he brought back a paper, saying, 'Today, we are going to discuss what being a true leader is. First, what qualifications does one need to be a leader? ... .' He is in the first grade! Kids at this age never talk about this kind of thing in Japan. I guess in Japan people see their leaders as one of them, or as mirror of their voice. But the American people see their leaders as individuals who actually 'lead' them. So the American people are more careful about how they choose their leaders than the Japanese. One last point about a problem that I have experienced with American presidential elections: the candidates pursue active electoral campaigns only in the 'swing states' – the handful of states that really could end up voting for either candidate. People in these states see many TV ads about the candidates and are more likely to see candidates visit their states to give a speech. I have lived in the United States almost ten years, but I have never seen active presidential campaigns, because I have always lived in 'safe states.' The people in those states are exposed to less information about candidates, and their votes do not affect the outcome of the election in the same way. Since the Electoral College process is what leads to the importance of swing states, the only way to fix that problem would be to reform the Electoral College."

CHAPTER 7

Legislative Process: Congress and the President
立法過程：議会と大統領

　アメリカの立法過程は動きが遅く混乱に満ちている。憲法における規定がこの動きの遅さの原因となっている。すなわち、議会と大統領との間の権力の分立、そして議会の中では上院と下院の間の立法上の役割の違いである。そしてそれらによって、立法過程に多くの拒否点（法案が成立するのを阻む機会）が生みだされるのである。上下両院では多数を形成するために、そしてそれを阻むために、政治的取引や党派政治が行われる。そしてそれが立法過程の混乱を引き起こすのである。本章ではアメリカで法律がどのように形成されるのかについて述べる。

President Donarld Trump making the State of the Union Address, 2019. It is one of the rare opportunities for the president to appear in Congress. Source: www.commons.wikimedia.org.

Lawmaking in the United States is a slow and messy process. The slowness is by constitutional design: the separation of powers between the Congress and the President, and the division of the legislative function within Congress between the Senate and the House means there are many veto points where potential laws (bills) can be killed before being born. The messiness is an inevitable outcome of political bargaining and partisan politics which facilitates and obstructs the formation of majorities in the House and the Senate. This chapter examines how American laws are made.

When the American President pushes for some legislation, he or she takes the strategy of "going public" to gain popular support. This demonstrates the nature of the American legislative process. The Japanese Prime Minister has less incentive to gain public support because he is usually selected by the majority in the Diet. Moreover, the Japanese executive branch, and more specifically the cabinet, can introduce bills to the legislative branch and the Prime Minister has chances to explain them in the Diet. By contrast, the American President has no power to submit bills in Congress and cannot come to Congress without invitation. Although bills go through the committees and are voted on the floors of the two houses in both Japan and the United States, the political dynamic of the legislative process is significantly different. In addition to the different role of the Japanese Prime Minister and the American President, coalition making in the legislative branch differs in the two countries because the political parties function differently, and because divided government is possible in the United States while it is not in Japan, with one major political party in control of one or both chambers in Congress, and the other party in control of the executive.

The President as Chief Legislator in the Separation of Powers

Right after an election, American Presidents feel empowered to push through a legislative agenda. Since they have just won a national election, their Party and the media will often interpret the electoral victory as a vindication of policy visions articulated during the electoral campaign. The inaugural address – the President's first speech to the American people – is an important medium through which a new president presents his ideas. Then, at the beginning of each of the three remaining years of his term, through nationally televised annual messages to Congress, the President continues to try to set the legislative agenda.

While members of Congress have primary responsibility for initiating legislation and managing the details of the legislative process, the overall policy objectives of Congress are significantly shaped by the President, with his stamp of approval. Except for the Speaker of the House of Representatives, whose selection is similar to how Prime Ministers in parliamentary systems are selected, the President can more than any other single actor, influence the broad policy

Signature of President Obama on the Patient Protection and Affordable Care Act. Presidents usually use multiple pens when signing a bill into law so that they can give them to their supporters. Source: www.lowademocrats.org.

goals of a particular session of Congress. Furthermore, each bill passed by both chambers of Congress will either be approved by the President to become a law, or be vetoed by the President to die. It is not an exaggeration to say that the President is the most powerful political figure in the American political system.

Although he has tremendous power, the President is far from omnipotent. He cannot, and usually does not, get what he wants. The framers of the constitution expected that the policy agenda of the President would diverge from the policy agendas of the Senate and the House. As James Madison and Alexander Hamilton wrote in Federalist Paper 51, the officers of each branch would be elected through "different channels" and their ambitions would counteract one another. In that respect, legislative gridlock means that the system of separation of powers and checks and balances is functioning as it was intended.

However, prior to the elections, the Democrats and Republicans formulate national policy goals. Therefore, if the executive and legislative branches are controlled by the same political party – what political scientists call unified government – the separation of powers becomes less separate, as the partisan connection enables the President and Congress to coordinate more effectively across the institutional divide. Because partisan goals effectively unify the aims of the President and members of Congress, there will be much less legislative gridlock when the same party is in power. By contrast, under divided government, the intended checks and balances of one branch against the other functions more effectively. When a President from one party faces a Congress controlled by the other, the party leadership in Congress normally tries to prevent the President from enjoying any political successes. They do this to lessen any positive impressions American voters might form of the leaders of the other political party. In addition, Presidential vetoes of Congressional legislation are far more likely under divided government than under unified government.

One last point about Presidents and their partisanship: political scientists debate the extent to which Presidents position themselves at the center of their party, or at the center of the American electorate. Upon taking office, most Presidents try to portray themselves as above partisan conflict. After all, there is no other actor in the American political system who can legitimately claim to represent a majority of the American people. On the one hand, there is no doubt that every President tries to reshape and rebrand the image of his political party. So, it is clear that he cares about the fortunes of his political party. On the other hand, Presidents are much more moderate than the center of their political party, and they have to be – especially during their first term, where the imperative to get reelected with the help of Independents and at least some members of the other party pushes them toward the middle of the political spectrum.

Furthermore, Presidents are highly sensitive to polling agencies such as Gallup, which manages a daily tracking poll of American adults, and which reveals the American public's approval or disapproval of the President's job performance. More so than other elected officials, Presidents need to respond more actively to national public opinion polls about matters of policy – like raising taxes on the wealthy. Unlike Senators and members of the House who are ultimately responsive to their much more limited constituencies, the President can suffer electoral defeat if he does not respond to national polling. While responding to the middle can alienate the President from elites and activists within his own party, it is a good strategy to take for reelection.

Lawmaking as a Collective Action Problem and How Congress Overcomes It

435 members of the House of Representatives and 100 Senators in Congress represent 310 million Americans. Each member of the House represents about 700,000 people. The constituents of a House member representing part of New York City live in a very small geographic space for such a large country. They are urban, cosmopolitan, racially, ethnically, and religiously diverse, and politically liberal. They have very different concerns and interests than the constituents of the single House member representing the entire state of Wyoming – a vast expanse of land, with mountains and plains, whose people are almost all white, and whose culture is relatively homogenous. Furthermore, the people of each of the 50 states live under the distinct laws of their state governments, and the different American regions – Northeast, Mid-Atlantic, South-Atlantic, Midwest, Southwest, Plains and Mountain States and the Pacific – all have distinctive political cultures and different balances of economic interests and occupational opportunities. All of this means that the 435 members of the House, each of them representing very different constituencies, will likely have very different policy agendas in Congress. If they only pursued the local and particular interests of their districts, it is easy to see how Congress would get very

little done. Policymaking for the nation as a whole would be very difficult indeed.

Political scientists refer to this potential for gridlock as a collective action problem. From this perspective, the fact that Congress and the President ever enact new legislation is a considerable organizational achievement. Consider just the House for now: how do 435 members with individual ambitions and very diverse constituencies ever form majorities in support of new legislation? Three factors coordinate the legislative process and make lawmaking possible: the committee system, political parties in government, and bargaining. First, the committee system coordinates a division of policy labor so that not every single member in the House has to know everything, or even anything, about each policy area that the national legislature will eventually confront, such as welfare, health, education, wars, energy, transportation, etc. With about 20 standing committees in the House, and each member serving on about three of them, members can focus on specific policy fields.

Second, every single member in the House belongs to either the Democratic or Republican parties, and the unified political agendas of the parties, and the party leadership institutions in the House, make it possible to form legislative majorities. Third, even though Members do think of themselves as partisans, they primarily think of themselves as responsible to the particular interests of their district constituencies. A Democrat in New York City is very different from a Democrat from rural Louisiana. While they might agree generally on the purposes of government and on many issues, they will likely disagree on others such as gun control and gun ownership, with the Northern urban representative favoring tighter gun control and the Southern representative from a rural area opposing it. Because of differences in their constituencies, partisan majorities are some-times difficult to forge. When that is the case, legislative bargaining, through which one member agrees to vote now on a bill he weakly opposes, so that he can get support from other members later for bills he strongly supports, facilitates the formation of a majority.

The Committee System

The United States Constitution permits the House and the Senate to organize their legislative activity as they see fit. From early on in the Republic, the members of Congress divided themselves into specific policy committees so that members could focus on specific areas of particular interest to them and their constituents. Over time, the number of committees has risen and fallen, with a peak number in 1940 of more than 80 committees in the House. In 1948, President Truman signed a law reorganizing Congress to make it more efficient. Since then the number of standing committees has been around 20 in the House and Senate.

In the House of Representatives, the number of members on each committee ranges from nine on the Committee on House Administration to 62 on the Committee on Armed Services, with an average of 40 members on each committee. Almost all the committees delegate their work to various subcommittees, with an average of 16 members. Through this division of policy labor, members can concentrate on specific policy areas of interest to their constituents.

Not all committees are equally powerful. In the House, the Committee on Rules is the second smallest committee with only 12 members, but it is one of the most powerful and the most partisan, with two thirds of its seats held by the majority Party. The Rules Committee has control over the legislative agenda in the House. It places bills on the legislative calendar to determine when floor votes on a bill will be taken; and it also controls the amount of time bills and amendments to them will be debated, and how much time

Bill Gates, the founder of Microsoft, testifying in a hearing before a Committee in the House of Representatives (2008). Source: www.house.gov.

any member is allowed to debate the bill. In contrast to the small Rules Committee, which is a highly partisan institution, are very large committees like the Committee on Armed Services composed of 62 members. The partisan composition of these large policy specific committees reflects the overall partisan composition of the House. In addition to making policy, the committee also functions as a patronage machine, with members whose districts contain military bases or arms manufactures trying to get on the committee in order to maintain federal spending for their districts.

Every committee has a chair, elected by the majority party, and a ranking member, who is the most senior member of the minority party. While every committee is certainly partisan – with committee members tending to vote along party lines when bills are referred to them for consideration, Congressional scholars also know that each committee has a subculture of its own, and it is not unusual for members to agree to legislation for patronage reasons, despite partisan disagreements.

Finally, each committee has familiar relationships with departments and agencies in the executive branch, a fact that is discussed further in Chapter 8. The members of the House Committee on Transportation and Infrastructure, for example, work closely with bureaucrats in the U.S. Department of Transportation, and they are lobbied heavily by the 50 state Departments of Transportation. Although there are certainly problems with how the committee system functions, it is hard to imagine Congress working without it.

Political Parties and Caucuses in Congress

The most powerful person in the United States after the President is the Speaker of the House of Representatives, who is second in line to be President should tragedy strike, and the President and Vice-President cannot serve, because of death or some other incapacity. A majority of the House elects the Speaker. Traditionally, the election of the Speaker falls along a party line vote, with all the members of the majority voting for the leader of their party, and all the members of the minority voting to elect the leader of their party. Although the Speaker is definitely a partisan figure, like Prime Ministers in Japan and other countries, and like the President of the United States, Speakers all start their office with pledges to be fair to the minority. Throughout their term, they try to court members of the other party whenever possible.

Speaker Nancy Pelosi (Democrat, California) delivered a speech about the American Rescue Plan on March 13, 2021. She asked for the public support for the bill. Source: www.speaker.gov.

Under a divided government, the Speaker has many incentives to avoid working with the President. However, to the extent that both officials want government to get things done, compromise with the other party is inevitable. Most Americans know very little about the Speaker of the House, failing to realize what a powerful and important position he or she holds. Periodic polling of Americans shows that fewer than 40% can name the Speaker. Unlike the President, Speakers tend not to be very public figures – except insofar as the opposition media demonizes them. Successful Speakers are excellent at keeping the members of their party together during key votes, and forging compromises with the leadership in the Senate and in the White House. Below the Speaker are the Majority Leader, a member of the same party, and then the Minority Leader, the top ranking leader of the minority party. When control of the House switches partisanship, it is common for the Minority Leader to become Speaker. Below the leaders of each party are the Party Whips. The primary job of the Whips is to make sure that enough members of the party vote together to advance the agenda of the party and to advance their electoral fortunes.

Political party leaders also maintain control of their members and the legislative agenda by raising money through political action committees – funds the leaders can distribute to their members to help in their reelection campaigns. Leaders also control the agenda by placing members who share the same priorities as the chairs of the committees discussed above. Party control over committees, however, is something that has varied over time. Sometimes senior or ranking members of committees are able to maintain control of committees even as the party leadership changes, with the preferences of the committee diverging from the political party agenda. When this occurs, tensions between the committee chairs and party leadership can become quite strong. Tensions may also emerge between committee chairs and party leadership because the experience and policy expertise of the committee members might diverge from the agendas of the party. Thus, the two major institutions in Congress that facilitate lawmaking and that help to overcome the collective action problem – the committee system and the party leadership – will sometimes clash.

One final important institution in the U.S. House of Representatives is the Caucus – an informal group of members with common ties and shared governing philosophies and policy vision. The caucuses organize without official recognition by the Constitution or even by the rules of the chamber, and they are not funded by the appropriations process. In addition to the major party caucuses, prominent partisan caucuses include the Blue Dog Coalition of conservative Democrats and a liberal counterpart, the Progressive Caucus. On the Republican side is the Tea Party Caucus of libertarian Republicans. In addition, there are ethnic and racial groups such as the Congressional Black Caucus and Hispanic American Caucus, and several non-partisan and policy-specific groups such as the Congressional Caucus for Women's Issues, the Law Enforcement Caucus and the Immigration Reform Caucus. While some of these caucuses have been around a long time, others come and go. Their purpose is to help members with common interests draft legislation and advance their common policy goals.

Legislative Process and How Members Vote

Many American citizens born since the 1970s remember watching a short cartoon music video by Schoolhouse Rock called, "How a Bill Becomes a Law." The main character is a rolled up piece of paper – a bill – who is stuck in committee and hopes someday to become a law. The truth is, the normal fate of most bills is that they die – and there are many ways to die (for the basic flow of the legislation, see Table 7). Once introduced by a member of Congress, a bill might never get referred to the committee of jurisdiction. And, if referred to a committee, it might never be reported out of the committee. And, once it gets to the floor of the chamber, it can die if a majority opposes it. If the bill makes out of one chamber, then it must

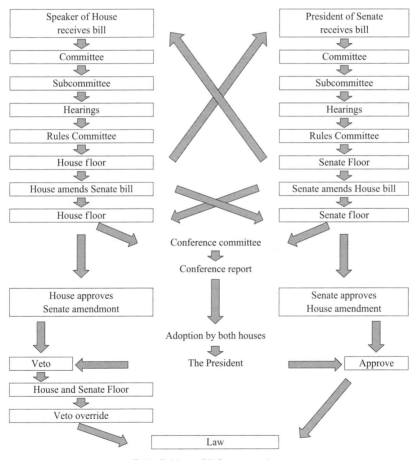

Table 7: How a Bill Becomes a Law

start the whole process again in the Senate, where it must be referred to that chamber's relevant committee, reported by that committee, and then supported by a supermajority of the members. Even at that point, the fate of the bill depends on the President's veto, discussed below.

Any member of the House or Senate may introduce a bill to the Congress. Usually the bill a member introduces was drafted by his staff, or by the staff of an official in the executive branch, or by an interest group who gets a member to sponsor the bill in the House or Senate. Whatever policy area is the main focus of the bill determines which committee the bill will be referred to for review. In the committee, members may amend the bill, and then a majority of the committee has to vote to report the bill back to the floor of the House. The committee's report on the bill may or may not recommend that the chamber consider further amendments to the bill. Once the bill comes out of committee, it is placed on the calendar of the chamber so the members of the Committee of the Whole, that is, a quorum of the total members of the house, can debate the merits and demerits of the bill and perhaps amend it.

In the House, how much time any member has to comment on a bill or argue for an amendment is strictly controlled by the majority party's leadership. In the Senate, where party leadership is much weaker, and where each single member has much more authority, any Senator can choose to argue for or against a bill for as long as he or she likes – what is called a filibuster. The filibuster is an old tradition in American politics, which has become a problem as the Senate increased in size. In 1917, the Senate adopted the "cloture" rule, which enables a supermajority of the Senate to vote to stop filibusters from going on for too long. The filibuster tradition and the high vote threshold for cloture makes it relatively easy for one Senator to stall the legislative process, and it means that a supermajority in the Senate has to act together to move the process forward. Many political scientists are critical of the filibuster for this reason.

At this point, however, even if the bill makes it past all of these hurdles, the bill might *still* not become a law, and its ultimate fate could be to die upon the President's veto. Or, if the bill passes near the end of the legislative session, it can die just by sitting on the President's desk without him signing it (a pocket veto). In fact, if you consider the number of bills that are passed into laws – between 1991 and 2011, about 221 bills were enacted each year – the number of regular vetoes, excluding pocket vetoes, is relatively small. From 1789 to 2012, there have been only 1500 regular vetoes, or about 7 vetoes a year, with some presidents exercising this power far more than others. For example, Thomas Jefferson vetoed no laws in eight years. Franklin Roosevelt, by contrast and in a much different political era, vetoed 372 bills during his time in office, or an average of 28 vetoes for each of the thirteen years he was President. More recently, President Barack Obama only vetoed 2 bills in his first term – in a Congress that enacted 383 laws.

It is important to note, however, that actually vetoing bills is not the only way the power of the veto is employed. The *threat* of a veto can be extremely effective too, leading Congressional leaders to revise parts of a bill they know the President will never support. Also, the President is unlikely to veto a bill that is extremely popular, since he will look weak if two thirds of both chambers in Congress vote to override the President's veto. So, veto politics entails strategic maneuvering in both branches. But, if the bill makes it beyond the veto stage and is signed by the President, it becomes a permanent law unless language in the bill specifies a date that its provisions will expire. Of course, the law can always be repealed by future Congresses. In addition, judicial review of the law by the Supreme Court, which could find the law in violation of the constitution, is always possible. Judicial review is discussed in more detail in Chapter 9.

For many political scientists, the most interesting moments in the legislative process are the votes on the floors of the House and Senate on amendments to the bills, and on final passage of the bills. Every single vote taken in the House is public; and any citizen can see how each member voted on a bill. The best website that presents this information is www.gov-track.us. Once the bill comes to the floor for the final vote, what structures how members voted? Political scientists have a plethora of data they can use to analyze – and predict – why members vote the way they do. They have detailed information about the personal characteristics of the members and about their ideological orientation, as measured by the entire history of their votes cast in many different policy areas. In addition, political scientists have information about the demographic characteristics of their constituencies, including the racial composition, religious diversity, ideological diversity, the influence of different economic sectors, etc. All of these factors help us to make sense of voting behavior.

On any vote, the following factors tend to matter most: partisanship, political ideology, race, gender, occupation, the region the congressional district is in (for example, South vs. Midwest), the wealth of the district, and committee membership. Partisanship can matter in positive and negative ways: it is common for the majority party in Congress to try to frustrate the legislative agenda of the President of the opposing party, such that even when individual members support a President's specific policy goal, they might vote against it any way, to prevent the President from looking successful. Political ideology matters too: every member of Congress is highly opinionated about the proper role of government, and they will tend whenever they can to vote in line with their genuinely held political beliefs.

But, more basic than their partisan bents and their ideological leanings is what political scientist David Mayhew calls the electoral connection: more than anything, members of Congress care about looking good to their constituents so that they will ensure their reelection.[1] Thus, if the majority of the people living in a Congressional district believe that the abortion of fetuses is a form of murder, it is highly unlikely that their member of Congress will ever cast a vote that can be portrayed by potential chal-

---

[1] While the President can only get elected twice, Congressmen have no term limit.

lenger as a vote in support of abortion. To do so would be political suicide.

Generally speaking, most members of Congress first and foremost view themselves as delegates representing the interests of the majority of their constituents – especially when the vote is on a bill that the media is paying a lot of attention too. However, every member of Congress also has his or her own personal convictions about what is best for their district, and for the nation as a whole – convictions that might come into conflict with what the majority of his or her district wants. In that case, the member gambles when voting with their conviction against what the district wants. Nevertheless, on issues that his constituency is not likely to hold very strong opinions about, he will most certainly vote his convictions.

So, on many votes the member of Congress behaves like a delegate – carrying out the interests of the constituency in a straightforward way. On many other votes, the member behaves more like a "trustee" of the common good of his district or the nation. And finally, on many other votes, the member behaves pragmatically, or what political scientists refers to as a politico: he votes in whatever way that will best ensure his reelection, or that will make it more likely that he can move up the power hierarchy in the committee system and within the party in Congress. Members of Congress will make sure that any vote they make now against the interests of their district, or against their own convictions, will be repaid later on by some other Congressmen voting vote against their interests. In other words, members of Congress behave strategically. And those strategies have big consequences. Their behaviors and their interactions with the President of the United States create laws and policies that will govern Americans for generations.

Lastly, presidential power in the legislative process depends not only on the political skills and personal charisma of the president, but also on the power of the executive branch. The power of the presidency has itself changed over time. During the 19th century, the presidents' influence was limited, except in cases such as national emergencies, such as wars and economic crises. However, the presidents' power over Congress significantly increased during the 20ᵗʰ century. Presidents gained power by increasing the capacity of the federal bureaucracy (see Chapter 8). The bureaucracy increased its size because the federal government was expected by Congress and the public to respond the economic and social problems (see Chapters 10, 11, 12).

Cross-Cultural Dialogue 7: Disapproval of the Government

Michael : "In October before the November 2012 presidential election, only 48 percent of Americans approved of the job that President Obama was doing. If you think that sounds low – the approval rating for Congress was even lower. Only 13 percent of Americans believed Congress was doing a good job! And, yet 93% percent of the members of the House of Representatives won reelection. Such a low approval rating combined with such a high rate of reelection is odd, but political scientists think they know what is going on. First, Americans disapprove of Congress because they don't like the high levels of partisanship in the House. Americans see their government failing to work well. But, when it comes to reelection time, Americans in each Congressional district tend to vote again for the representative, especially when he or she pushes a partisan agenda that pleases the particular constituency. Do you see similar kinds of puzzles in Japan, when in one breath people view the government as failing to get things done, and in the next breath, they reelect the same people to office?"

Taka : "I think there is the same phenomenon in Japan, though it is now less than during the period when the Liberal Democratic Party was a dominant force in Japanese politics for a long time after the war. People are frustrated with the performance of the Diet, but when elections come they tend to vote for the same legislator  because he or she provides benefits for them, bringing jobs and subsidies to their district. But the situation in Japan is more complicated than in the United States. In the United States, the members of the House of Representatives are expected to work for in the people's interests of their districts (the average population is about 700,000); Senators represent for their state; and the President for the entire nation. In contrast, the Japanese electoral system is too difficult for many people to understand! The House of Representatives of Japan, for example, adopts a system of single-seat constituencies and proportional representation. To make it more complicated, one who loses in the single member district could win in the proportional representation scheme, depending on how narrowly he or she loses. Moreover, many people do not fully understand how the Prime Minister is elected. Although this system has good aspects, such as protecting small parties, voters and members of the Diet are confused about what interests they are voting for and what interests they work for, respectively. I think this difference between the two countries results partly from their different concept about the public interest. While Americans think compromises among regional, racial, ethnic, religious and other interests lead to the public interest, Japanese try not to define divisions in our society much in order to reach the public interest."

CHAPTER 8

Bureaucracy
官僚制

　日本人とアメリカ人が政府官僚という言葉を聞いたら、両者は別々のイメージ
を思い浮かべる。日本人は、官僚は高い専門性を持つ尊敬すべきエリートである
と考えることが多いだろう。他方、アメリカ人が最初にまず思い浮かべるものの
一つに、自動車庁（Motor Vehicle Administration）である。そこは主に自動車免
許の手続きのために行く場所であるが、長い待ち時間と劣悪なサービスで有名な
のである。アメリカ人は、公務員の仕事が民間企業の仕事よりも社会的地位が高
いとは必ずしも思っていない。このように日米両国民が政府官僚に対する異なっ
た態度を持つのは、両国の異なった政治文化だけでなく、政治システムやその歴
史的発展の違いが背景にある。

Civil Service Reform. *Harper's Weekly*, 1877 March 31. This shows the old days when
the Presidents appointed his friends and supporters as the government officials. But by
the end of the nineteenth century, it appeared that this corrupt system could not stand
anymore. In the drawing, people are begging the statue of Andrew Jackson for their jobs in
the federal government. The bottom reads, "St. Jackson, can't you save us? Can't you
give us something?" Courtesy of the U.S. Library of Congress.

When people in Japan and the United States hear the term "government bureaucrats," they have different images in their minds. The Japanese people are more likely to think that bureaucrats are admirable elites with great expertise. By contrast, one of the first things that the American people come up with in their minds is the Motor Vehicle Administration, the office where you go to get your driver's license, and which is known for very long lines and bad service. Americans do not necessarily think that being a public servant is a superior job, in terms of social status, to working in private business. These different attitudes toward officials in government result not only from the different political cultures of the United States and Japan, but also from the different political systems and their historical development.

In Japan, among the 1,326 people who passed the exam for the Main Career Track National Public Service in 2020, 249 were graduates from the University of Tokyo. The top five universities – Tokyo, Kyoto, Waseda, Hokkaido, Tohoku – sent 35.1% of successful candidates. Many graduates of the prestigions universities also chose to work as officials at the prefectures and municipalities. The public service has been one of the dream jobs for many Japanese students. By contrast, in the United States, becoming a government official is not usually one of the jobs on the wish-list for many graduates. Most American graduates look for jobs in the private sector. Professor Matthew Crenson at Johns Hopkins University, one of the top American universities, voiced the regret of many academics when he said, "Students here study political science, but not many of them try to get a job in the government. There are some who go into careers at the federal level, but there have been only a few students who got jobs at city hall in the past ten years." This difference in attitudes toward government officials between Japan and the United States results in part from the different political systems of the countries.

American Bureaucracy in the Separation of Powers

In Japan, the majority of the Diet elects the Prime Minister. The executive branch has the power to introduce bills in the Diet: it introduced more than 80% of the entire bills after the Japanese Constitution was enacted in 1947. The government bureaucrats, unelected officials working under the Prime Minister, make this happen. Therefore, the bureaucrats write, introduce, and implement policy. In Japan, there are many critics who argue that the bureaucrats have too much power, but the system makes it possible.

In contrast, as Chapters 1 and 2 described, the U.S. Constitution created the federal government with many limitations. The Constitution, with the separation of powers and federalism, was designed to prevent one person or institution from becoming too dominant of a power. However, as Chapter 4 indicated, the enumerated powers of Congress have been an important basis upon which the power of the federal government has increased over time. Nevertheless, the President has a limited power to shape policy, compared to its Japanese counterpart. The executive branch has no direct power to introduce bills in Congress. Constitutionally speaking, while congressmen have the authority to write, introduce, and pass bills in Congress, the federal bureaucrats deal with the policy implementation process.

When the Constitution was written, the biggest fear of colonials was that unelected federal officials would make important decisions without representing the interests of the people, as the British King had done to them. The Constitution has no provisions for bureaucracy. But, even if not specifically noted, the Cabinet was created by the following words in Article 2, Section 2: "[The President] may require the Opinion, in writing, of the principal Officer in each of the executive Departments, upon any subject relating to the Duties of their respective Offices." The Cabinet was composed of the senior members, usually heads of the executive branch. Furthermore, Article 1, Section 8 empowered Congress to do everything "necessary and proper" to carry out its enumerated powers, such as raising taxes. The combination of these clauses led to the formation of executive departments like the Treasury Department.

Thus, each executive department and the officials working within them were created by bills to assist the Secretaries as they execute their duties. The federal government started with only three small departments – State, Treasury, and War (which became Defense after World War II). It is important to note here that unlike Japan, which abolished the feudal Tokugawa Shogunate by reviving the tradition of *Ritsuryo-sei* bureaucracy, the United States was founded by politicians and they later created the bureaucracy. Therefore, politicians take an initiative to make policies in the United States. Having elected officials be in control of bureaucrats is what the Democratic Party of Japan proposed, *seijishudou*, when it became the majority party in 2007. But it has not overhauled the tradition.

Limited and Non-Professional Bureaucracy

As time went on, the size of the federal government and the number of federal officials grew. But these increases did not result automatically in the rise of the bureaucrats' power. Rather, the limited power of bureaucrats was due to the fragmented political system and the patronage system that developed in the early 19th century. The spoils system, also known as the patronage system, was adopted by President Thomas Jefferson (1801-1809) and was widely expanded by President Andrew Jackson (1829-1837).

When Thomas Jefferson was elected as the President in 1800, he removed the federal bureaucrats who served under Presidents Washington and Adams, who leaned toward the Federalist Party. Then he appointed men who shared his republican political views of limited government. This turnover of officials between the second and third American presidents created the tradition that many bureaucrats were removed when a new president came in office.

Andrew Jackson advanced the nature of the patronage system with his own political philosophy. He was the first president who was not in the elite class and who identified himself with the "Common Man." He believed that the power of the federal government should be limited not only by keeping its size small, but also by using common citizens instead of elites to staff the government, and by rotating those officials frequently so that none of them were in power for too long. When he came into office, he placed his friends and supporters in the federal government bureaucracy posts. Many of them had little policy knowledge and political experience. Jackson believed that he could prevent corruption and make the federal government more responsible to the people by giving the government posts to non-elites.

Jackson did not like the centralization of national power. He vetoed renewal of the National Bank (the Second Bank of the United States) because he thought that it would give too much power to one institution, to rich people, and to Congress. However, he did not always oppose the quantitative expansion of the federal bureaucracy. For example, he expanded the size of the United States Postal Service, which was created as a department under the George Washington administration. By the time Jackson became the president, the population had increased and many Americans had settled in the western states and territories. He expanded the post offices and appointed many of his supporters as postal employees. For him, a federal government staffed by common men as officials would be safer for the American democracy. With the common man in government, the government would be less likely to serve the interests of a wealthy financial elite.

Calls for Civilian Service Reform

Jackson's amateurish bureaucracy was capable enough to survive in the middle of the nineteenth century. The federal government's job then was simple and its responsibility was limited mostly to improving interstate infrastructure and setting tariffs on imports. But it became widely known that when the new administrations took office, job seekers rushed to Washington, D.C. to get jobs, and many of them were untrained for their positions or, even worse, disinterested in the jobs they got. Moreover, in contrast to Jackson's hope, the spoils system became a source of bribery and corruption. As the federal government's responsibility gradually grew, reformers emerged to ask for changes. They claimed that the spoils system should be replaced by a merit system that hired new federal employees not because of their partisan loyalty to the president but because of their ability to do their jobs well, as measured by passing competitive exams.

Scandals of the Ulysses S. Grant administration (1869-1877) fueled the movement to introduce the merit system. Many cabinet members and federal bureaucrats allegedly engaged in briberies and corruption. Interior Secretary Columbus Delano was forced to resign after it was discovered that he took bribes for land grants. Secretary of War William W. Belknap also resigned from office by taking the blame for taking financial favors from the tradership contract of Fort Sill. Other scandals included briberies and other misconduct by federal bureaucrats and Grant's personal secretaries. This series of scandals widely demonstrated that the spoils system was an incompetent system that needed to be reformed.

The opportunity for civil service reform came with a tragedy. In September 1881, after serving in office for only four months, President James Garfield was shot fatally. Charles Guiteau, the assassin, was disappointed because he was rejected for an ambassador position which he thought he deserved because of his support for Garfield in the presidential election. The assassination reminded the public about the necessity of civil service reform, and Senator George Pendleton took a lead to pass the Pendleton Civil Service Reform in 1883, which introduced a merit-based federal civil service. This new system initially applied to only 10 percent of federal employees. But soon, most of the federal bureaucrats began to take competitive exams. Expertise was now more appreciated than personal ties with politicians.

From Serving to Regulating

The introduction of the merit system was a response not only to the bribery scandals and the presidential assassination but also to the changing nature of the federal bureaucrats' tasks. The federal bureaucracy used to be the institution to serve the people, like the Postal Service. But in the late nineteenth century, it

Scene of President Garfield's assassination at a train station in Washington, D.C. Drawn by A. Berghaus and C. Upham (1881). Courtesy by the U.S. Library of Congress

began to play more of a regulatory role in the economy.

The creation of the Interstate Commerce Commission in 1887 as the first regulation for industry demonstrated part of the scheme change. It initially targeted the largest interstate railroad firms, like the St. Louis and Pacific Railway Company that nearly monopolized the market with few competitors. The Commission empowered the federal government to intervene in the railroad industry to achieve reasonable and just rates for transporting cargo on the trains, if not to directly set specific rates. The Sherman Anti-Trust Act of 1890 was a further involvement in the economy

"The administration hardest job" by J. Leppler. T. Roosevelt and his fellow administrators are trying to calm down a donkey named "democracy." Courtesy of the U.S. Library of Congress.

for the federal government. It gave the federal government the authority to investigate corporations if they monopolized the market or attempted the monopolization.

The regulatory role of the federal government rapidly increased under the Theodore Roosevelt administration (1901-1909). He identified the federal government as the protector of the free market and more aggressively utilized the Sherman Anti-Trust Act to bust large monopolies, or "trusts" as they were called. But there was still a fear among Americans about the expansion of bureaucratic power. The further expansion of the federal government had to wait until an unprecedented economic downturn that began in October 1929.

The Expansion of Bureaucracy

Franklin D. Roosevelt's administrations (1933-1945) further increased the size and role of the federal bureaucracy. In response to the Great Depression, the federal government expanded its role in the economic regulation of agriculture and industry. The main goals of regulation were to maintain the appropriate supply and prices of products, and also of wages. The Agricultural Adjustment Act of 1933, for example, provided subsidies to farmers if they reduced production, thus preventing the price slump. The Public Work Administration, which was created by the National Industrial Recovery Act of 1933, also dealt with public projects to boost the employment. To plan and administer new programs, the federal government increased its capacity by hiring thousands of officials in newly created positions and dramatically increasing federal expenditures.

Roosevelt's political program promised a "New Deal" for Americans, and included the expansion of social policy, such as the Old-Age, Survivor, and Disabilities Insurance and the Unemployment Insurance. While the development of social policy increased the welfare of the people, it also resulted in a sharp expansion of the federal bureaucracy. The federal government had to hire more bureaucrats to administer these new programs. This expansion continued during World War II and the postwar period in the name of the war mobilization and the postwar reconstruction, respectively. In the 1960s, Lyndon B. Johnson pushed the trend further with his political promises to create a "Great Society," which included new public programs to combat poverty, improve education, and promote health care (see Chapter 12).

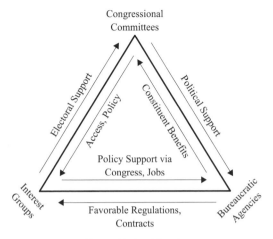

Figure 8.1: Iron Triangle

The initial growth of the federal bureaucracy was mostly a response to the economic and social problems. But once it began to develop, some critics argue, the federal bureaucrats became allied with narrow-minded interest groups and members of Congress on related policy committees to drive the expansion of the programs further. Political scientist Theodore Lowi argues that "Iron Triangles" among the interest groups, congressional committees, and executive agencies is the mechanism that pushes for programs' further expansion (Figure 8.1).

For example, a subsidy program for farmers is decided in the Agricultural Committee of the House of Representatives that is composed of congressmen from districts in which agriculture is a major sector of the economy. They were elected with the support of agricultural interest groups. Both the congressmen and the interest groups cooperated to ask for the expansion of the subsidy program. The Department of Agriculture that deals with the program administration also has a stake in the program because funding for the programs provides the Department with its budget and personnel. Because of this Iron Triangle, the critics argue, whether programs effectively work or not, the expansion of the programs per se sometimes becomes their top priority of the stakeholders. This political dynamism takes place in any country with a democratic political system, including Japan.

Hugh Heclo offers a different, but complementary, perspective to understand what kind of role the American bureaucracy plays in the policy-making process. Heclo emphasizes that policymaking is not only driven by the narrow interest of stakeholders. Rather, a loose network of experts, or what he calls an "Issue Network," affects policy changes. This network is based on the relationship that people develop as they work together over time, and stay in contact over the phone, emails, and texts. Issue Network participants, Heclo argues, consider wider interests than the Iron Triangle theory assumes.

The unique aspect of Issue Network, at least to the Japanese audience, is that the network includes actors outside the federal bureaucracy, such as congressional staffs, policy aids to congressmen, policy consultants working for industry and special interest groups, journalists, think tank researchers, and academic researchers. In Japan, the important policy information is concentrated more in the few officials in the central government. The power of think tanks is also limited. New policy ideas typically come from the central bureaucrats.

The "Revolving Door"

This openness of the policy formation process in the United States resulted partly from the legacy of the spoils system. The merit system extended to many positions in the early twentieth century, but high official positions are still held by political appointees, selected through the partisan process of presidential nominations and Senate confirmations. The recent administration changes have caused the turnovers of between 3,000 to 4,000 political appointees. Many top officials in the former administration then work as high paid policy consultants for special interest groups, think tanks, and universities, and they continue to have influence on policy formation.

This may remind some Japanese of *amakudari* – "descent from heaven" in the direct English translation - by which top officials get influential positions in the public and private sectors after they retire. But the American phenomenon is different from *amakudari*. Remember that the American top officials were appointed by the President for their political support and policy expertise. They were not the career bureaucrats who worked their way up to the top positions. Although some career bureaucrats are turned into political appointees, the political appointees usually work in the private sector before taking high-ranking positions. When a new administration comes to power and fires them, which typically happens when there is a change in the political party of the administration, the fired employees will usually find jobs outside the federal government. Then, later on, when the candidate of their party who they support becomes the President, they seek jobs in the federal government again. "Revolving Door" is the term used to describe this rotation of the personnel between the federal government and the private sector. On the other hand, when Japanese officials take positions in the private sector after their retirement, they have less incentive to study new policies because they have no chance to get back to the government positions.

One criticism of the Revolving Door is that it creates a cozy relationship between the federal government and the private sector because many top officials in the regulatory agencies have had or will have jobs in the regulated industries. To prevent the close relationship from becoming a hotbed of corruption, agencies have ruled that the former officials are not allowed to contact their former workplace about the policy matters for a certain period.

The Revolving Door system also leads to inconsistency and frustration among bureaucrats within the bureaucracy. When the new administration comes and the new top officials take offices in a department, all the career bureaucrats were expected to follow the new policy direction. The policy change is usually wider when the opposite political party takes the presidency. This circumstance makes policy implementation inconsistent.

Moreover, the career bureaucrats in the United States are not the same as *kyaria kanryo* in Japan. The latter could have a large influence by becoming chiefs of bureau and eventually Administrative Vice-Ministers. But in the American system, it is harder for career bureaucrats to rise to the higher positions occupied by political appointees and to become more influential. The American career bureaucrats face a clearer ceiling that brings frustration to them, and there tends to be a deeper division between them and the top officials, who are political appointees.

The radical development of the federal bureaucracy in the twentieth century caused a governance problem of "too big to control." Simply put, the Presidents and even top officials in the departments cannot grasp everything. They are more likely forced to make decisions based on the insufficient information provided by the career bureaucrats. Moreover, although the Secretaries of departments are expected to work for the President, they represent the interests of their departments as well. The interests of the departments over which the Secretaries do not have a full control often conflicts with the interests of the President.

The President vs. the Bureaucracy

The power of the bureaucracy comes not only from its size but also from its discretionary power. The reason why the Articles of Confederation did not include an executive branch was that people feared that the bureaucrats would implement policies that would distort what the legislative branch intended. The second half of the twentieth century witnessed not only that. It also

Figure 8.2: The Structure of the Executive Branch

saw that the President often could not be responsible for what bureaucracy does in the policy implementation process.

To solve these problems, the President expanded the Executive Office of President (EOP) that works directly for the President. The EOP staffs usually have easier access to the President than their counterparts have in the departments. While the latter work for their Secretaries, the former directly report to the President. The EOP includes the White House Office in which many policy advisors assist the President. It is widely known that President Richard Nixon trusted and worked much more closely with Henry Kissinger, his National Security Advisor in the EOP than he trusted or worked with the Secretary of State William Rogers, in the foreign policy formation.

The EOP includes organizations to coordinate the departments. For example, the National Security Council that was established in 1947 includes the President as chair, the Vice President, Secretary of State, Secretary of Defense, Chairman of Joint Chiefs of Staff and many other top officials. The National Security Council was created as a tool not only to coordinate multiple departments but also to make the policy process closer to the President.

While some Presidents have made more effort to have the bureaucracy under their control, others have more seriously tried to reduce the size of the bureaucracy. Ronald Reagan (1981-1989) sought to cut the federal government budget, except the defense budget, and sought to abolish the Department of Education. Reagan wanted to abolish the federal education department, not because he believed that education policy was unimportant, but because he believed that state government should be responsible for education policy.

Federal Bureaucrats and State Bureaucrats

Reagan's conservative response to the growth of the federal bureaucracy raises another characteristic of the American federal bureaucracy, which is related to policy in a federal system. As was discussed at the end of Chapter 4, the federal bureaucrats share functions with the related state government officials. Unless the authority is explicitly delegated exclusively to the federal government, like national defense and coinage, the state governments could counter the federal authority. For example, the state governments have large discretion on education policy (see Chapter 10). This is different from the Japanese bureaucracy. Bureaucracy at the prefecture-level serves more like a local administrative branch of the central bureaucracy and it has much less discretion on many policy areas.

Going back to the first contrast made at the opening of this chapter, while the career bureaucrat is considered a good career in Japan, very few graduates from well-known universities in the United States hope to enter a career as federal bureaucrats. In the United States, the career federal bureaucrats have less power to write bills, to implement laws, or to guide public policy. One reason is that the career bureaucrats have to work under the political appointees, who have great access to the top decision makers such as the President, while the career bureaucrats themselves have very little access. Moreover, and more importantly, the American fragmented political system results in more actors who can influence the policy process than exist in Japan's more centralized system. Therefore, even political appointees in the U.S. usually cannot capture as much power as the top government officials in Japan. Finally, the idea of the small federal government echoes much more strongly in the United States, where there is a strong political culture of citizens who suspect that the bureaucracy is too big and that bureaucrats are gaining too much discretion in the policy process. Ironically, even though American bureaucrats are relatively powerless, Americans have a stronger tradition of viewing them as having too much power.

Cross-Cultural Dialogue 8: In Praise of Bureaucrats?

Michael : "American English does not have a simple, positive sounding term that refers to career government officials. But, it does have a term which has become almost a dirty word: the 'bureaucrat.' Many Americans do not view the officials who work in the federal bureaucracy as admirable public servants with great expertise – rather, they view them as soulless robots undermining American freedom. Americans have developed a negative mythology about the 'bureaucrats' who work in government. Bureaucrats in this mythology are not your neighbors, but a distant powerful force: they file lots of paperwork; they do what it takes to expand the budget of their departments; and in their mostly boring existence, they take pleasure in writing rules that they can impose on the rest of us. Probably, most of the people who go into government do so because they want to serve the national good, and because they have the expertise and positive ambition to make a difference – but that is not the way many Americans see it. To what extent are Japanese critical of Japanese bureaucracy? And, if they are generally less critical than Americans, what do you think explains why they have a more positive view of government officials?"

Taka : "After seeing inefficient works by the government officials, many Japanese people are also upset and say, 'This is a typically bureaucratic way of working!' Also, people's trust has declined because of reports in the media that the bureaucrats take advantage of their positions and waste tax money for unnecessary purposes.  But as the university ranking story at the beginning of this chapter suggests, people still know the government officials are drawn from the best and the brightest. Many young people, including my students, take the exam for public service to serve the national or local good. But the flip side of the people's trust in the government officials is that the people partici- pate less in the policy discussion and they rely too much on the bureau- crats for the course of public policy – ultimately the future of the nation- than their American counterparts. But I do not think that the American sit- uation is healthy, either. In the United States, it seems to me that everyone speaks up without thinking about making compromises. Which is better for a country to have: people's great trust in the bureaucrats and little interest in politics, or people's little trust in the government and selfish pursuit of their own narrow interests? Of course, I like somewhere in between. But how to make that happen is a very difficult matter."

CHAPTER 9

The Supreme Court and Judicial Review
最高裁判所と違憲立法審査権

　アメリカの司法府の最高機関は合衆国最高裁判所である。建国期には、新憲法に反対する者たちは、選挙で選ばれない者たちで構成される最高裁の権力が時代とともに強大になることを警戒していた。他方、新憲法の支持者たちは、連邦の司法府は（他の二府に比べ）常に「最も危険性が少ない」機関であるとした。すなわち、アメリカの自由を侵す可能性が最も少ない機関であるとしたのである。現在、政治に関心を持つ者の多くは、最高裁が強大な権力を持っている機関であると考えている。違憲立法審査権を行使することによって、最高裁は議会や大統領のリーダーシップによって通過させた法律を、9人の判事のうちの多数が違憲であると判断することで葬り去ることができる。本章は、最高裁の権力について説明し、そして最高裁がどの程度政治的、党派的機関になっているのかについて述べる。最後には、最高裁判事が議会が成立させた法律の合憲性を判断する時に用いる法を解釈する上での2つのアプローチについて言及する。

Protestors outside the Supreme Court of the United States as the Court was deciding the constitutionality of President Obama's health care law, the Patient Protection and Affordable Care Act. June 2012. Photo by Takakazu Yamagishi.

At the top of the judicial branch of American government is the Supreme Court of the United States. When the country was founded, the opponents to the new Constitution worried that the Supreme Court, with its non-elected members would become too powerful over time. The supporters of the Constitution argued by contrast that the federal judicial branch would always be the "least dangerous" – that is, the least likely to be a threat to American liberties. Today, most political observers agree that the Court is a tremendously powerful institution. With the power of judicial review, it can overturn laws passed by Congress and the president that a majority of its nine members believe are unconstitutional. This chapter explains this power of the court, and addresses the extent to which the court is a political or partisan institution. Finally, it introduces the two main legal approaches that members of the Court employ when they assess the constitutionality of laws enacted by Congress.

In Japan, the 15 members of the Supreme Court with a retirement age of 70 are nominated by the cabinet and appointed by the emperor. Then the National Review for Judges of the Supreme Court is held when the next election of the House of Representatives takes place. As described in this chapter, the selection procedure of the Supreme Court Justices in the United States is quite different. Among other things. the selection process is much less politicized in Japan than in the United States. In Japan, news media do not usually report much on the new judges. But in the United States, the selection process, especially over the last three decades, tends to be longer and cause much more political controversy. The differences result from the different position of the Supreme Court in the political system and the different development of the judicial branch.

Thinking about the Role of the Supreme Court

The United States has thousands of judicial courts. Each state has its own hierarchical system of courts, with city and county courts at the bottom, appeals courts above them, and a State Supreme Court at the top. Many Japanese people may be surprised to learn this, but in most states, the judges of the courts are elected by the people, usually through non-partisan elections (the image is a campaign poster, or sign board, for a judicial candidate). Because of these elections, judges at

Campaign Sign of Mark E. Mitchell, state judge in Georgia. Courtesy of Mark E. Mitchell.

the local level are often viewed as neighbors in the community in which they live. Given this, the American people's attitude toward the judiciary is different from many Japanese people's attitudes.

Elected judges normally have much longer terms than officials in the executive and legislative branches of government. At the state and local levels, courts deal with criminal (violent infractions) and civil issues (non-violent crimes and contracts). The State Supreme Courts have authority to interpret the state constitutions. When Americans go to court – to settle disputes over contracts, to dispute a traffic ticket for speeding on a highway, for example – they go to courts organized within the states. So, the state and local courts are certainly important.

This chapter, however, focuses on the federal judiciary – the system of courts that deals with national political issues and American constitutional law. The federal system is organized hierarchically, with 94 districts courts spread around the 50 states and American territories, with each state having at least one district court, and few more depending on the population. Above the district court level are 13 appellate or circuit courts that receive cases appealed from the district courts within their geographic region. At the top of the federal system is the Supreme Court of the United States, composed of eight Associate Justices and one Chief Justice. The Chief Justice of the Supreme Court is the highest-ranking judge in the

United States.

The Supreme Court of the United States wields tremendous political power. However, the nature of judicial power differs from the legislative and executive powers commanded by the two partisan branches of government. The U.S. Constitution clearly states that Congress has the power to make new laws, which includes the power to tax and spend the income and wealth of the people of the United States. The President has the executive power to direct the bureaucracy and the armed forces of the United States. By contrast, the federal judiciary – the Supreme Court, the 13 appellate courts below it, and the 94 district courts below them – cannot create new laws and they need the executive and legislative branches to enforce their decisions.

The Supreme Court's role, according to the current Chief Justice, John Roberts, is that of an "umpire": it allows the other two political branches of the federal government and the state governments to make law and implement policies as long as they do not break the rules laid down in the Constitution. In other words, the federal judiciary has the power to declare what the constitution means, and whether any federal, state or local laws violate the Constitution. The Supreme Court, of course, has ultimate authority should there be any disputes over the meaning of the constitution in the lower circuit or district courts, or should the members of the Supreme Court disagree with the lower court holdings.

This power to review the legislation enacted by the elective branches of government is called judicial review. Surprisingly, that power is not given to the Court in the constitution. Rather, the Supreme Court asserted this power in *Marbury v. Madison* (1803), when it overturned a part of the 1789 Federal Judiciary Act. That Act empowered the Court to command officials in the executive branch to enforce laws dealing with the judiciary. However, the Constitution did not give the court any powers of enforcement – that power belongs to the executive branch. In the case, William Marbury was appointed by the outgoing federalist president John Adams to be a Justice of the Peace. When Adams' political foe, the Democratic-Republican Thomas Jefferson became President, his Secretary of State, James Madison, refused to keep the appointment, and so Marbury sued Madison. Marbury petitioned the Supreme Court to command Madison to make the appointment, and the Court's response was tremendously important.

Chief Justice John Marshal presented a very clever ruling: he found that by the Judiciary Act, a federal law, Madison did owe Marbury his appointment – thus, avoiding taking sides in the partisan conflict between Adams and Jefferson. But, he also said that the Judiciary Act itself was against the Constitution and that his Court could not command Madison to deliver the appointment. Marbury had to give up his job, but the precedent of judicial review was established by this case. Although the Constitution did not give the Court the

A lithograph of Chief Justice John Marshall, by William Henry Brown (1844). Courtesy of the Library of Virginia.

power to overturn acts of Congress, in this important case, the Court simply asserted it had that power, and since then, the Court has used it. Without this case and without more than two centuries of court activity based upon its principle, the Court's authority would be very weak today.

When thinking about the role of the Supreme Court in the American political system, it is important to ask how much the Court behaves like a political institution, reflecting partisanship and democratic public opinion. Alternatively, it is important to consider whether the court makes decisions in a formal legal way that is somehow beyond political pressures. Judicial review of legislation involves interpreting what the Constitution means and analyzing the intent of legislators who enacted the laws under examination. But, is interpretation a political act? Legal scholars disagree on whether judicial interpretation is more like an umpire enforcing the rules of a base-ball game, or it is more like a committee who is rewriting the rules of the game.

Political scientists argue that the court is not a purely legal institu-tion; rather, political motivations shape many aspects of the Court, from how the members are appointed, to the gate-keeping process that deter-mines which cases the Court will hear, to the arguments laid out in its majority and dissenting opinions. Nevertheless, even as politics shapes the Court, many Americans are taught in school to be in awe of the Court, and to respect it as a non-political institution, a team of guardians safeguarding the Constitution rather than a team of partisans who use it to advance their own partisan goals. The ceremony of the court, including the priest-like robes the members wear, and the high bench they sit behind during legal proceedings, contributes to this aura. This view of the court, however, has changed dramatically over the history of American politics. Today, a slight majority of Americans do in fact view the Court as a partisan institution.

Yet, the members of the Court do not think of themselves as political partisans. Rather, since most of them are in fact experts of the law and members of a legal profession, they view themselves as non-political offi-cials, and are happy to describe the judicial philosophies and methodological approaches of legal interpretation that guides their decision-making. Unlike the partisan legislative process described in Chapter 7, which is shaped by the desire of members of Congress to be reelected, and by their responsive-ness to interest groups, the members of the Supreme Court will say they act only on the basis of legal reasoning, and always with reference to legal precedents. And they view the Court as a highly constrained institution, which is supposed to be isolated from the democratic process; not an active one that is supposed to be highly responsive to it. Whether or not a majori-ty of the American people supports the laws the Court reviews has only a small impact on how the Court will rule.

And, the sad truth is that while most Americans understand the

Court's importance, very few can name the current Chief Justice, and even fewer pay attention to its decisions – even highly publicized ones like the recent 2012 case, which examined the constitutionality of President Obama's signature health care legislation, the Patient Protection and Affordable Care Act. Furthermore, the elaborate rulings of the court are difficult for most American citizens to comprehend because they are written in legal language and refer constantly to legal precedents with which most Americans are unfamiliar. For students of the American constitution, however, Supreme Court cases are fascinating works of political theory and political philosophy and are highly rewarding to read. Finally, although the Supreme Court alone does not have the power to alter the path of American history, there is no doubt that it has played a major role in doing exactly that.

How the Court is Political

Members of the Supreme Court are nominated by the President and are confirmed by a majority vote in the Senate. Prior to confirmation, nominees testify before the Senate Judiciary Committee as Senators try to assess their judicial philosophy (described below). The hearings are good political theater – far more likely than the not, the Senate will confirm the nominee. Some political scientists argue that the primary function of the hearings, as with most Congressional hearings, is to allow Senators an opportunity to display their own toughness and ideological convictions that would please their constituencies. But these hearings are not just a good show: the legal approach justices take does make it more or less likely how they would rule on many important issues that could come before the court, especially those dealing with the rights of citizens, and the proper role of the federal government in the American political system.

Once nominees are confirmed as a Supreme Court Justice, they hold their seats for life or until they retire or are impeached. The current Court has six members appointed by Republican presidents: President George H. W. Bush appointed Clarence Thomas in 1991; Brett Kavanaugh in 2018,

George W. Bush appointed Chief Justice John Roberts in 2004 and Samuel Alito in 2005; and Donald Trump appointed Neil Gorsuch in 2017, Brett Kavanaugh in 2018, and Amy Coney Barrett in 2020. Democratic presidents appointed the four other justices: Bill Clinton appointed Stephen Breyer in 1994, and Barack Obama appointed Sonia Sotomayor in 2009 and Elena Kagan in 2010. Although all nine of the current justices are trained lawyers with prior experience as judges, there is no requirement that Justices be lawyers or have had any experience serving on a judicial bench. In fact, one of the most famous Chief Justices in American history, Earl Warren, who sat on the Court that issued *Brown v. Board of Education*, the 1954 case that desegregated American public schools, was a former Governor of California who had never served a day as a judge.

There is no question that the political party of the President who appoints a justice is related to the way the Justices rule on cases. One piece of evidence for this is that most of the split decisions of the Court reflect the partisan origins of their appointments. The members of the Court, and

Front row, left to right: Associate Justice Samuel A. Alito, Jr., Associate Justice Clarence Thomas, Chief Justice John G. Roberts, Jr., Associate Justice Stephen G. Breyer, and Associate Justice Sonia Sotomayor. Back row, left to right: Associate Justice Brett M. Kavanaugh, Associate Justice Elena Kagan, Associate Justice Neil M. Gorsuch, and Associate Justice Amy Coney Barrett. Source: www.supremecourt.gov, accessed on July 25, 2021.

especially the Chief Justice, would prefer all of the decisions to be unanimous – with all nine justices agreeing in a given case that a particular law does or does not violate the United States constitution. Unanimous decisions are rare; much more common is a majority of six, seven or eight members, with the remaining members dissenting. But split decisions – where five members support the majority opinion, and four members do not – happen frequently enough, and get so much media attention when they do occur, that the public image of the Court has been undermined in the last three decades, as Americans increasingly view the Court as a partisan institution.

Split decisions also make clear that the constitutional issues at stake in a review of the law are far from clear: if five members say the law is constitutional and four say it is not, that suggests that there are multiple ways to interpret the law's constitutionality. The losers in such Court cases may take some comfort in that ambiguity: should the composition of the court change in the near future, it could be that the new members could tip the balance of the court to overturn the previous ruling. This possibility occurred in October 2012, when the Supreme Court took on a case that assessed if racial affirmative action policies at universities violate the American constitution, by giving unequal preferences to racial minorities. Only nine years earlier, the Court with a different membership had ruled such affirmative action policies were constitutional. Given that the current majority of the court is appointed by Presidents who opposed affirmative action, it is quite possible the Court will now find that race based affirmative action policies do in fact violate the constitution. A reverse ruling like this tells us at least one thing: even though the constitution rarely changes, the Court's interpretations of it do, tracking changes in the court's membership.

There are two other ways in which the Court operates like a political institution: how it selects the cases it will review, and how it anticipates how other actors in the political system will respond to its decisions. First, the process by which appealed cases from lower courts make it to oral arguments and hearings before the Supreme Court is based on the issue preferences of the individual Justices and their legal clerks and staff. The Supreme Court receives about 8,000 petitions a year from parties who would like the Court to consider their appeals. But, the Court only accepts around 80 of those each term for actual review. So, only 1% of all cases that are appealed to the Court actually make it into the Court for review.

The decision making process that rejects 99% percent of most cases and selects 1% of them for actual review in the Court is not random. It involves legal considerations about the merits of the cases, and assessments about which of the cases would have a greater impact on clarifying controversial constitutional issues. The law clerks are, for example, more likely to select cases for review if circuit courts below the Supreme Court had arrived at different conclusions about the constitutionality of the law in question. In other words, the Supreme Court likes to select cases where its decisions will be important. But more significant than all of these legal factors, is the fact that cases are selected because the members of the Supreme Court have an interest in them. For example if one of the Justices has a particular interest – intellectual, personal, partisan – in an issue, such as protecting gun rights, he will press his clerks to bring any gun right cases that appear among the thousands that are sent to the Court to the top of the pile for consideration by the Court. In this way, the personal or political preferences of the individual justices have an effect on constitutional law, and the decisions of the Court. These personal biases can have a great impact on Americans' rights and liberties.

Finally, even though the members of the Court would like to make their constitutional decisions purely on the merits of the case, and purely on the basis of whether the particular federal or state law they are reviewing is objectively supported by the U.S. Constitution, or objectively violates it – the decision-making of the Court does not happen in a political vacuum. The Court is quite aware of what goes on in the political world of presidential politics, Congressional bargaining, electoral pressures on government officials, and of American public opinion. More importantly, it is quite aware of how its decisions will affect electoral politics, and the Court's own reputation with the American public. Generally speaking, the Court is reluctant to take on cases that will result in decisions that go sharply against popular laws passed either by state legislatures or by Congress. When American public opinion is strongly behind certain laws, the Court does not enjoy ignoring it. When the Court does rule against popular opinion, it incurs the label of being an activist Court that has traded in its legitimate constitutional role as an interpreter of the law, for an illegitimate role of making its own laws. However, even though most decisions do not go against public opinion, Americans tend to remember the cases where the Court did go against public opinion – as when the Court desegregated the public schools in the South, or when it discovered that the privacy protections that the Bill of Rights extends to American citizens should extend to women's privacy in making decisions about her own body and health, including the decision to have an abortion. The fact that these are the rare cases, not the common ones, does not change the increasing view of the court as an activist institution that is not sufficiently deferential to the elective branches of government.

Judicial Review and Interpreting the Constitution

The 111th American Congress (2009-2011) which met during the first two years of Barack Obama's presidency, enacted 383 public laws – excluding "private laws" which do not apply generally to the nation, but specifically persons or states, and treaties, which are legal documents in international affairs. Only one of these – the Patient Protection and Affordable Care Act – was subjected to the Supreme Court's power of judicial review. While opponents of the law argued that the U.S. Constitution did not give Congress the power to require individuals to pay a tax penalty if they failed to get health insurance, the President's administration and supporters of the law argued that the Constitution *did* give Congress that power. So, the American people wondered: "Does the new health care law violate the

Constitution, or is it permitted by the Constitution?" And reasonable citizens could sit down with the Constitution and look at what it says, and then look at the health care law and see what it requires, and then come up with reasonable answers of their own. But of course, their answers do not have the force of law. Only the federal judiciary – the justices of the district and appellate courts and ultimately of the Supreme Court – has the authority to declare what the constitution means.

So, does the health care law violate the constitution? In the majority opinion of the Court, which 5 of the 9 justices agreed with, Chief Justice John Roberts argued that most of the law does not violate the Constitution, while some parts do. In order to reach that decision, the Chief Justice has to interpret the Constitution, and decide whether the meanings of specific clauses in it, can support what Congress and the President were trying to do with the health care law. It's important to remember that judicial review of law is always an act of interpretation, and there are several approaches Justices take as they interpret the Constitution.

Justice Antonin Scalia, appointed by the Republican President Reagan, and Justice Stephen Breyer, appointed by the Democratic President Clinton, are well known for their two different approaches to interpreting the Constitution. Legal scholars call Scalia's more conservative interpretive approach "Originalism" and Breyer's more liberal interpretive approach, the "Living Constitution" approach. Both these approaches have a common goal: to constrain how they decide whether the authority the federal and state governments assert when they enact a new law or implement a rule are permitted by the Constitution. But, the logical rules they follow to make this judgment are different. Scalia argues that interpretation of whether a law violates the Constitution should be constrained by the original meaning of specific clauses in the Constitution. His interpretive goal is to recover what the authors or framers of the Constitution meant when they wrote, for example, that Congress will have the power to "regulate … commerce among the several states." The original meaning of the framers should be referred to when deciding on the constitutionality of a law or rule.

By contrast, Breyer with his living constitution approach factors in the consequences on democracy the decision will have, and argues that interpretation should be guided by a very different set of criteria. The key to Breyer is his argument that constitutional interpretation is a matter of treating the document as a whole; a document that supports broad principles of democratic participation, active liberty, and individual dignity. Then when he is ruling on whether or not a given law violates some clause of the constitution, he asks a question: "If I declare the law unconstitutional, will I diminish equality of citizenship, or democratic participation?" If his answer to such a question would be yes, then he will be less willing to declare the law unconstitutional – he wants to make sure his decisions promote democratic participation, not undermine it. For Breyer, the consequences of his decision are paramount in how he makes a decision.

Furthermore, because ideas about who should be citizens have changed over time, and ideas about what the proper role of the state is as society has become more complex has also changed over time, Breyer argues that Justices should guide their judgments with a practical understanding of those social changes. To take the health care law as an example, for Breyer, an important fact to consider is how the nature of commerce in the American economy has changed over time. When the framers decided on the language that Congress will have the power to regulate commerce, they almost certainly did not mean the power to regulate health care. However, today the provision of health care amounts to one sixth of the entire American economy, which is certainly a whole lot of commerce. For Breyer, whether the framers could have imagined this change to the economy is less relevant than how elected officials today try to address it, as long as the expanding power of Congress is not unreasonable.

It is important to note that although Scalia's approach is more conservative, it is not old-fashioned, or necessarily out of date. His main argument is that Justices should recover what the authors of the specific clauses of the Constitution meant, and that original meanings should guide the Justices' interpretation. If the First Amendment to the constitution is being interpreted, then, according to Scalia, you have to figure out what the authors who wrote it in 1789 meant when they wrote it. But, if the twenty-sixth amendment to the Constitution, which gave 18 years olds the right to vote in 1972 is being interpreted, then justices have to examine what people in 1972 meant. And if tomorrow, the American people amended the constitution to ensure that all Americans have access to health care, then he would say that to interpret that new amendment, we would have to look at what the American people in 2013 meant when they brought about that amendment. For him, it is really about who has the power to make law. Generally speaking, he wants to make sure that the authors of constitutional language govern the meaning of that language, and not the Justices of the Supreme Court, whose job in his view is simply to police and enforce those original meanings. In Scalia's view, if a Justice does not constrain his interpretation by those original meaning, the Justice is simply substituting his own ideas about what the Constitution should mean for what the authors of the clause intended it to mean. And, when justices do that, they are overstepping their authority and are usurping the legislative function of government away from the People.

Although there are clear differences between these two approaches, the truth is that all Justices use elements of the approach they prefer less. Breyer certainly takes into account the original meanings of the text in his decisions. And, Scalia certainly allows the meaning of certain words to reflect changing circumstances. For example, on the question of what exactly is the Second Amendment right that Americans have to "bear arms" (or weapons), all Justices would acknowledge that the right originally had something to do with empowering citizens to protect their states from foreign threats (an originalist finding). In addition, they would all concede that a reasonable protection of that right today must take into account that guns

	Scalia	Breyer
Names of approach	Originalism, Literalism	Consequentialism, "Living Constitution"
When interpreting the Constitution ...	Recover the original meaning of the text of the constitution. What the framers meant by words at the time they wrote them is what the Constitution should mean today.	Maximize "an active and constant participation in collective power" and the "dignity of the individual." Allow original clauses to adapt to changing circumstance.
Criticisms of other approach	Leads to subjective assessments about what the constitutions should mean. Judges are not supposed to make the Constitution mean something new. Ignores that only state Legislatures or Congress have the authority to change what the Constitution says or permits.	Offers no guidance on how to judge the law in the face of changing societies. Fails to use the Constitution as a practical text offering guidance on how to judge the constitutionality of new laws. Limits the potential of the ideals in the constitution that promote democratic participation and the protection of individual liberties.

Based on Antonin Scalia, "Common-Law Courts in a Civil-Law System: The Role of United States Federal Courts in Interpreting the Constitution and Laws," *The Tanner Lectures on Human Values*, Princeton, University (1995), and Stephen Breyer, *Active Liberty: Interpreting our Democratic Constitution* (New York: Alford Knopf, 2005).

Table 9: Two Supreme Court Justices' Approaches to Interpreting the Constitution.

today are much powerful and much more dangerous and deadly than they used to be (a living constitutional finding).

The justices take these legal approaches to interpretation very seriously, and if more Americans became more familiar with them, perhaps they would be less likely to view the Supreme Court as a partisan institution. And yet, even as Americans have increasingly blamed the Court for being guilty of making highly partisan rulings, there remains a remarkable deference to the Court once it has presented its decisions to the public. As the picture at the beginning of the chapter illustrates, when the Court does its business, American citizens are not at all shy about letting the Court know their opinions. Just as there were many protestors urging the Court to uphold President Obama's health care law, there were also many protestors who urged the Court to overturn the law. When the Court eventually read its decision to the press, supporters of the law were elated and celebrated how the Chief Justice, who was appointed by a Republican President, apparently reached a decision beyond partisanship. By contrast opponents of the law were terribly disappointed, and many decried Chief Justice Roberts as a sort of traitor to conservative Republican ideology. Despite these partisan reactions and despite the great emotions on both sides of the law, eventually the drama of the Court faded from the public view, the rule of law prevailed, and the fate of "Obamacare" was placed back in the political arena of elections.

Cross-Cultural Dialogue 9: The Role of Judges in a Democracy

Michael : "I've always been struck by this strange position of the Court in American democracy: we Americans expect the Court to be above the partisan fray, but any time the court reaches decisions that conflict with our partisan views, we blame the Court for being too political. What the judges actually do – write legal decisions – is very different from what the President or members of Congress have to do – build public support and legislative majorities to get laws enacted. The Court is supposed to be wise and just follow the law, and ignore the passions of the people. But that doesn't stop people from protesting outside the Court to make their opinions known, and it doesn't stop people from hoping the members of the Court will pay attention. What was the atmosphere outside the Court like when you took the picture at the beginning of the chapter? Does such a scene ever occur outside the Japanese Supreme Court? If not, why not?"

Taka : "I was in front of the Supreme Court when it released its decision on the health care reform, or what is often called 'Obamacare.' It was crazy! Many people rallied to raise their voices for or against the health care law. The legislation has a huge impact on the American economy, society, and politics because health care occu-  pies one-sixth of the American economy and health care touches the people's lives from their birth to death. To me, it was exciting to witness that the Supreme Court made a decision on such an important law. Also it was so interesting to see Americans feeling that the Supreme Court is part of democracy. When I felt the passion of the people in front of the Court, I reconfirmed that I was from a country in which the people, for better or worse, do not see the Supreme Court as an active institution, compared to the executive and legislative branches. At least, not to the same degree that Americans do. It is partly because the Japanese Supreme Court has avoided making clear decisions on difficult political issues, such as the constitutionality of the National Defense Forces. In addition, as we can see in Chapter 2, the Japanese people's overall attitude toward their constitution is different from Americans' attitude. Americans are more likely to think the Constitution is a core of their country while Japanese are not. If the Japanese Court re-interprets the Japanese constitution, therefore, it doesn't affect Japanese national identity nearly as much. But when the American court weighs in, like in the health care law, the decision reshapes American national identity and that stirs up the passions more."

CHAPTER 10

Family and Education Policy
家族政策、教育政策

　治安の維持やコミュニティーの繁栄や安定を元々守っていたのは、連邦政府で
も州政府でもなく、市、タウン、郡などの地方政府であった。地方の政策決定者
は、これらの社会の基盤を作るために家族と学校という二つの社会制度に注目し
た。そして彼らは婚姻関係や育児、そして子供への基礎的な教育についての法律
を作った。革新主義の時代（1900 - 1910年代）や公民権法運動（1940 - 1970年代）
以降、家族や公共教育に対する州政府や連邦政府の影響力が格段に増加した。し
かし未だ、アメリカの連邦制においては、異なった州に住むアメリカ人は、異
なった家族の在り方や子供の教育に関する法律の下で暮らしているのである。

Theodore Roosevelt Senior High School in Des Moines, Iowa built in 1922. The
beautiful architecture reflects the city's aspirations for their young adults who attended this school. Courtesy of the U.S. Library of Congress.

Originally, local governments in cities, towns and counties, and not the state or federal governments had primary authority securing the stability and prosperity of American communities. Concerned about the very basis of American society, local policy makers focused on two social institutions – the family and the school. They created laws to shape marital relations and child care, and elementary education for children, and secondary and higher education for young adults. Since the Progressive Era (1900s–1910s) and the Civil Rights movement (1940s–1970s), the influence of the federal government over the family and public education has increased. Nevertheless, because of American federalism, Americans living in different states live under different laws and rules governing their family lives and the educational opportunities for young people.

If the following two situations ever happened in Japan, Japanese people would certainly think they were very strange. First, imagine a same-sex couple who lives in Aichi Prefecture. Then, imagine that their prefecture does not legally allow same-sex marriage, while the next prefecture, Gifu Prefecture, has recently made it legal. So, the couple decides to move to Gifu and to get married there. Second, imagine a family with a ten-year old child in elementary school. They decide to move from Tokyo Metropolis to Saitama Prefecture, because the father got a new job. When they get there, they find out that the schools in Saitama require their child to study a very different curriculum. Although these two situations sound unrealistic and they would likely never happen in Japan, these differences in family possibilities and schooling opportunities are very common across the United States.

Because of American federalism, and in comparison to Japan, governance of many domestic policy areas varies a great deal across the American states and locales within each state. Generally speaking, the federal government in the United States has less authority than state and local

governments over family policy including marriage and childcare, and public education, than the national governments of most nation-states have. As
a result, the laws governing the family and public education vary across the
American states. In addition, within states, public education varies considerably across urban, suburban and rural places within the same state. As we
trace below, local and state policies regarding the family and the school
have changed a great deal since the nineteenth century as policymakers
responded to broad social changes caused by industrialization, urbanization
and immigration. Furthermore, over the course of the twentieth century,
the federal government became more involved in each of these policy areas.
However, in comparison to the large and significant increases in the federal
role in areas of economic policy, social security policy, and foreign policy
discussed in the following three chapters, the federal role in governing the
family and education has been much more limited, though also significant.

Finally, as with many political developments in the United States,
socioeconomic class divisions, race and ethnicity, and gendered social relations, along with ideological disagreements between the two major political
parties have structured changes in how these policy areas are governed. In
fact, the Democrats and Republicans not only respond to these issues in different ways; they also use the issues to distinguish themselves from one
another, and to build attachments between voters and the party that are
based on social identities. Examples of how American social diversity and
partisanship shape policymaking in the areas of family law and education
policy are discussed below.

The Family

American family law grew out of eighteenth century British traditions of marriage. American legislators, lawyers and judges crafted family
polices based on William Blackstone's Commentaries on the British common
law system. Marriage and family law in England rested on three pillars:
civic patriarchy, property and religion. First, the law asserted that women
were subordinate to men within the marital relationship, and that within a

marriage, women's legal identity was "covered" by her husband's. Legally speaking, she ceased to exist as a person under the law, with no rights to own property, to sue or to get a divorce. Second, one purpose of marriage and family law was to promote the orderly inheritance of property. Any property belonging to women would become the property of her husband when they got married, and any property accumulated by a family would belong to the male head of household, and could be distributed to his male heirs during his life, and inherited by them upon his death. Third, marriage and the family were based on the religious traditions of the Anglican Church, itself an offshoot of the Roman Catholic Church and the traditions of the European Protestant Christian sects. Marriage and having a family with children were understood to be an obligation of good Christian men and women.

What emerged over time in the United States was a "patchwork" across states of marital and family laws that drew upon these traditions. In most states, Americans are married in a religious ceremony, while their marriage is also registered with a county or city office. Thus, for most Americans, marriage primarily has a religious meaning, but the state governments have always regulated marriage, supporting it and the family as a civil institution. Furthermore, for all of the nineteenth century and most of the twentieth, marriage and family was also based on a system of racial segregation: in all Southern states and in many Northern states, marriage between men and women of different races was illegal. Until recently, states did not sanction homosexual marriage either, a fact that is discussed more below.

The marriage of President Grover Cleveland, aged 49, to Frances Folsom, aged 21 in 1886. Courtesy of the U.S. Library of Congress.

The purpose of the heterosexual family – and the

social roles that the dominant society expected husbands, wives and their children to perform within the household, in the economy and in the political sphere – have shifted dramatically over the course of American history. Prior to the industrial revolution in the middle of the nineteenth century in the United States, the typical family was economically supported by working parents and working children. On the family farm, husbands, wives and children all worked to support the household. However, as the economy industrialized and began to produce enough wealth to fund schooling; and, as children increasingly spent their time in schools rather than on the farm or in factories, the economic model of the family altered. Although both husbands and wives continued to work in lower class families, in the middle and professional classes, husbands worked outside the home, while most women did not enter the labor market, even as they remained engaged in the civic life outside their homes and in their communities, and their children spent more and more time in schooling.

Changes to the Family, 1900-1990

During the first decades of the twentieth century and the end of the Progressive Era, most mothers stayed at home doing work while their children went to school for only a few months out of the year and worked for the rest of the year – thus replicating the farm life in the urban setting. "Maternalist" policies, such as child labor laws and mother's pensions mentioned in the next chapter that were enacted by state governments and eventually the federal government, sought to protect children and support deserving single mothers, and to protect wives and children through the prohibition of alcohol. States also enacted compulsory education laws and then tried to regulate the problem of students who skipped school as a way of managing family relations and changing patterns of adult and child work. As the economy prospered, children could withdraw from the economy more easily, and by 1940, 73% of 14-17 year olds attended school. But things began to change after World War II.

After World War II, for the first time in American history, a near majority of married couples with children fit the stereotypical model of the father earning wages sufficient to support his whole family while his wife stayed at home managing the household and caring for the children. The middle class family model of the male "breadwinner" and the housewife at home with children in school until they graduated from high school became a cultural "norm" that many Americans aspired to fulfill. However, that arrangement did not last long for most American families. While in 1950, 47.1% of children lived in a house with the father in the work place and the mother at home, that that number had fallen to 26.3% in 1980. Within a couple of decades after World War II, most mothers combined working at home and child care with earning wages outside of the home, and in 1970, for first time in American history, more than 50% of married women worked outside the home. A large majority of these women worked part-time for lower wages than men earned, because employers expected that they would put family before work when they needed to.

Women's increasing role in the economy was also the product of the "second-wave" of feminism during the 1960s and 1970s, which may be compared to the "first wave" of feminism during the 19th century. Feminists during the first wave demanded formal equality under the law, including the right to sue in court and initiate a divorce, and to vote in elections and hold office in government. Second wave feminists, built on the successes of the first wave. They wanted to secure women's equal economic opportunities in the work place through laws guaranteeing equal wages, and securing greater control over their economic lives, which for many women, included having much greater control over when they would bear children. Supreme Court decisions during the 1960s and 1970s, including the 1973 Roe v. Wade decision, helped to secure a women's right to contraception and struck down state laws that banned abortions. With women's greater economic freedom and with the changes to married men's and women's participation in the workforce, new models of the family have emerged. In some, both parents now work and share the responsibilities of childrearing;

in others the single parent works and tries to manage child care arrangements with other family member or with financial assistance from the state and federal governments.

As the historian Cynthia Harrison has documented, these changes to women's participation in the labor force led to policy responses from state and national political actors, and especially lawmakers in the Democratic Party. In 1960, President John F. Kennedy's administration created a commission to investigate the conflicting roles of wife and mother, and to make policy recommendations to provide support in managing those different roles. In 1963, Congress passes the Equal Pay Act, which made it illegal for private employers to discriminate against women during hiring and in reviewing job performance and setting wages. Federal actors also created the Equal Employment Opportunity Commission (EEOC), which provided a federal venue through which women could bring a suit against private employers who violated the Equal Pay Act. The National Organization of Women formed in 1966 to make sure the EEOC did its job.

As more and more women entered the workforce, policy makers began to address the problem of how families with two working parents or single parent households would care for their pre-school aged children while the adults were at work. In 1971, Congress passed and the Republican President Nixon vetoed the Comprehensive Child Development Act, which would have subsidized childcare for poor families. The failure to enact that policy did not bring an end to the problem, however. In 1981, conservatives during President Reagan's administration enacted tax-credits that allowed families to pay lower taxes on their incomes depending on how many children they had.

Changes to the Family since 1990

In 1990, Republican President George H.W. Bush signed the "Act for Better Child Care" which provided funding to states for childcare services and tax breaks for mothers at home. The first major policy designed to help families care for their new born children without having to worry about losing their jobs was the Family and Medical Leave Act, signed into law by the Democratic President, Bill Clinton in 1993. This policy ensures that parents can take off up to three months of work to care for new children or to take care of other family members. While the law requires employers to reserve the jobs of employees taking family leave, the employers are not required to pay the employees during that time off. This policy, while a great help to many American families, provides much less aid than in Japan. In Japan, working parents are entitled to take three months off from work at 60% pay, and may take off the rest of the first year at 40% pay.

Working with a Republican Congress in 1996, President Clinton signed into law a major reform of income assistance to the working poor, including to poor working parents, the Personal Responsibility and Work Opportunity Reconciliation Act (also discussed in Chapter 12). As Cynthia Harrison has pointed out, a major purpose of the law was to promote the institution of heterosexual marriage, and to discourage single parent households. For example, in the Congressional committee report recommending passage of the law, the committee wrote that "Marriage is the foundation of successful society" and that the aim of the law was to "increase flexibility of States to provide assistance to needy families so that children may be cared for in their own homes or in the homes of relatives; to end dependence of needy parents on government benefits by promoting job preparation, work and marriage [and to] encourage the formation and maintenance of two-parent families." A heterosexual model of the marriage was certainly imagined by the authors of this legislative language.

In the same year, the same national political actors responded to the legalization of gay marriage in Hawaii, by enacting the Defense of Marriage Act (DOMA), which did two things. First, it asserted that the federal government would only recognize marriage as a union between one man and one woman, and that the term "spouse" for the purpose of assigning benefits to the domestic partners of federal employees would only apply to persons of the opposite sex from the employee. Second, DOMA declared that states which did not recognize same-sex marriage as legal did not need to recognize the marriage of couples who moved to their state from a state where they had been legally married. Opponents of DOMA argued in federal courts that the law violates the 14th amendment rights of all citizens to be equally treated under the law.

In 2012, Barack Obama became the first president of the United States to declare his support for homosexual or gay marriage, and his inaugural address at the beginning of his second term in 2013 was the first to link gay Americans' struggle for civil rights with the historical struggles of women and racial minorities seeking social and political equality. Conservatives in Congress, however, strongly opposed gay marriage, and most supported an Amendment to the United States Constitution that would define marriage as between one man and one woman.

Gay marriage was legal in some states, while it was banned by the state constitutions in many others. A few states permitted civil unions between gays, an institution that was supposed to confer all the rights and

Two men marry, surrounded by wedding party, in New Orleans, LA on November 11, 2017. Source: www.commons.wikimedia.org.

privileges that heterosexual couples enjoyed under the law – tax benefits, visitation rights in hospitals, the inheritance of property to children – but without calling it a "marriage," which again for most Americans was a term with a religious meaning. In several states, the state supreme courts have overturned anti-gay marriage laws. This created a tension between popularly elected legislators who campaigned on maintaining the sanctity of marriage, and liberal members of the courts who viewed the laws as a violation of equal treatment under the law. The American public though, is became increasingly tolerant of gay marriage.

In June 2013, the Supreme Court struck down Section 3 of DOMA. Edith Windsor, who lost her wife Thea Spyer in 2009, was the plaintiff. They were married in Canada and moved to the United States. Edith was forced to pay $363,053 in estate tax on Spyer's estate. She argued that she would not have had to pay if their marriage had been legally recognized. The court argued, "DOMA violates basic due process and equal protection principles applicable to the Federal Government."

Public Education

The ability of parents to work during the day and the arrangements they make to care for their children is obviously structured by the education laws of the states, which make available schools and teachers who educate American youth while their parents and guardians are engaged at work. Like the history of the American family, the political development of government's role in supporting and managing pre-school, primary, secondary, and higher education has also varied across the states. However, the basic purpose of schooling and the basic structure of administration have looked similar across the states, especially since the 1920s when high schools (secondary education) became common in the United States. Schools have also looked more similar as a result of increased involvement of the federal government following the Civil Rights movement, and important legislation that come out of it, such as the Elementary and Secondary Education Act of 1965.

The oldest public schools in the United States were established by law in the colony of Massachusetts, for religious and moral reasons: the Puritans of the colony believed that literacy was essential for all members of the colony, so that they could read the Bible. Many of the framers of the constitution argued the new national government should have a strong interest in the education of citizens. This was a political argument grounded on republican principles – that citizens of a Republic could not be both ignorant and free. With these ideas in mind, the Confederation Congress of 1787 included a famous education provision in its "Northwest Ordinance" – a law regulating how the Western territories would be settled: "Religion, morality, and knowledge, being necessary to good government and the happiness of mankind, schools and the means of education shall forever be encouraged."

Changes to Public Education since the Civil War

After the American founding, public schooling systems were created in the Northern states as the result of vigorous lobbying by prominent educators and politicians such as Horace Mann. No primary public schooling existed in the Southern States until after the Civil War, but by the turn of the twentieth century, all states had public schooling systems open to all races, though the quality of schools varied significantly within the racially segregated system. A United States Bureau of Education was created in 1867 to provide information to officials across the states on how best to create financial support and administer the system of public schools.

By 1918, all states had enacted some form of "compulsory education law." But, it is important to point out that these laws only compelled parents to ensure their children received basic levels of education – *not* to send them to a *public* school. They could get their education in a church school, or a private school, or even at home. While the public education system in the United States is very old, so too is a large system of private schools, most of them affiliated with some religion. Most of these are "parochial schools" operated by Catholic churches. In addition to religious schools are many privately funded schools, and in most states, "home-

Boys and girls in school, making patterns with teacher (circa 1910). Teaching was the most common occupation for educated women a century ago, and today it remains one of the most common for women. Notice how the boys and girls are all doing the same activity, regardless of their sex. Courtesy of the U.S. Library of Congress.

schooling" children is an option for parents, too. American law has always permitted families considerable freedom in choosing what kind of education – public, private, or at home – their children will receive.

Interestingly, the political development of primary and higher education during the late 18th century and the 19th century spread across the states during the same historical timing, while the development of secondary education, or "high schools," came later, and not until the first decades of the 20th century. There is a historical logic to this timing: education reformers wanted to insure that all citizens were basically literate and numerate – the purpose of the primary schools – and that those who excelled in academics, and who wanted to go into the professions of law, medicine and the ministry, would have a place to pursue their education – the purpose of colleges and universities. The oldest colleges and universities in the United States were founded through public and private partnerships, including Harvard College (1620), the College of William and Mary (1621), and other schools that now make up the "Ivy League" including Yale and Princeton. The University of North Carolina was the first state funded public university to be created after the Founding. Within a century, every state had established institutions of higher education.

To serve the small number of people attending these institutions of higher education, several college preparatory schools formed and were called "high schools," which offered an intellectually higher form of education than the primary or grammar schools. By 1920, most states had universally available high schools (see photo at the beginning of the chapter). As these high schools were created, more than one hundred thousand local primary districts were consolidated into a much smaller number of districts, each of them centered on a high school serving a large geographic region. Although many colleges and universities are much older than the high schools, broad growth in enrollments at colleges and universities only followed growth in attendance at the high schools. Enrollments at higher education institutions then grew immensely after World War II, when Congress enacted the "G.I. Bill," which among other things provided veterans of the War with money to go to college.

More than any other area of public policy, public education demonstrates the complex political relations in the American federal political system, and how those relations have changed over time in the direction of an increased role for the federal government. In 1920, there were more than 120,000 local school districts with some states having more than 5,000 districts each; today that number has been vastly reduced to around 16,000 districts today – still a very large number by international standards.

Each district is governed by an elected school board and administered by a superintendent, who is typically appointed by the board. The local school board in the United States has wider discretion than its Japanese counterpart. It has primary authority over raising taxes, hiring teachers and establishing the curriculum, but its discretion is limited by a system of education laws enacted by the state legislature. The state laws, however, tend not to be very detail specific – rather, they provide broad guidelines for how many days out of the year schools should be in session, what subjects should be taught in class, what qualifications teachers should have, and the process of hiring and firing teachers. The legislatures have also enacted laws establishing a funding floor for the public schools, and a funding maximum.

Urban school districts can be very large – with thousands of teachers and hundreds of thousands of students. With those large populations comes considerable racial and ethnic diversity. Suburban and rural districts, by contrast, will have many fewer teachers and students, and their populations tend to be very homogenous ethnically and racially. Thus, it is still common today for many schools to have large majorities of non-white students, and for many schools to be nearly all white. Although states may no longer enact laws to maintain racially segregated schools – as they did prior to the Supreme Court decision in *Brown v. Board of Education* (1954), American schools continue to be highly segregated by race because Americans tend to live in neighborhoods with other Americans of the same racial and cultural backgrounds. In fact, schools are more segregated now than they were thirty years ago.

While all school districts have considerable autonomy, they also must conform to state and national standards because of regulations implemented by departments of education in the state governments and by the U.S. Department of Education. The state departments are well established and old institutions, with most of them created in the nineteenth century. How these departments are governed varies across the states; in some they are governed by elected State Superintendents; in others the state superintendent is appointed by the Governor and confirmed by the state legislature. This officer is typically a career educator who is on friendly terms with teachers and teacher organizations. However, their selection to office depends on support from the business community, and on people with a lot of property: in most states, the property tax is the primary instrument used for funding the public schools.

Despite varying education policies by school districts, interestingly, almost all of them use this type of yellow school bus. Photo by Takakazu Yamagishi.

The Federal Role in Education

In contrast to the state departments of education, the U.S. Department of Education is a much more recent creation: with strong backing from the

National Education Association, the country's largest organization of teachers, and with support from officials in the state departments of education, the Democratic President Jimmy Carter and Congress created a cabinet-level department of Education in 1979. Since its creation, teacher's organizations have been one of the largest and most influential supporters of the Democratic Party. The Republicans tend to oppose increased spending on public schools and public school teachers, which they view as a form of political patronage that benefits a key element of the Democratic coalition. Their plans for "school choice" or "vouchers" – which would take funding away from the public schooling systems and give it to parents to spend on any school of their choice, including private schools, have little support from the teachers' unions. Republicans are also ideologically opposed to the U.S. Department of Education, whose existence they believe has no constitutional basis. Since Ronald Reagan's campaign for president in 1980, abolishing the U.S. Department of Education has been an important part of Republican presidential politics.

The creation of the U.S. Department of Education followed several decades of increasing federal involvement in the American public schools. The first major act of Congress relevant to public education was the Smith-Hughes Vocational Education Act of 1917. The Democratic President Woodrow Wilson argued that the federal government should support students who plan to go into the vocations, rather than into the professions: that is, into industrial and other lines of work, where the value of higher education in the liberal arts and sciences was not clear. The next major step toward a federal role came in the 1950s with the Supreme Court's decision to desegregate the public schools, followed by President Dwight Eisenhower's decision to use the National Guard to enforce the desegregation policies of the Court (see Chapter 4). Eisenhower also pushed Congress to appropriate funds for educational programs essential to the National Defense – especially, science, technology and the foreign languages.

The most important Act of Congress that dramatically altered federal relations, though, was the Elementary and Secondary Education Act of 1965, which has been renewed several times since then, and most recently as the "No Child Left Behind" law of 2002. The original ESEA provided funds for schools in poor areas, and required state legislatures and the state departments of education to comply with desegregation orders in order to get the funds. Amendments to the law have profoundly increased the edu-

cational opportunities of American racial minorities, and also American women, whose admission and support in colleges and universities were required by provisions of the laws.

President Bush signs the No Child Left Behind law. Source: www.whitehouse.gov.

No Child Left Behind included major policy changes that had bipartisan support, many of which are now loudly criticized by both parties. Democrats do not like how the law requires all schools to demonstrate yearly progress on test scores, or how it "punishes" schools in various ways, including state takeovers of the district if they fail to do so. Republicans do not like how the law has created more rules and regulations for local districts to follow. One reform that has some bipartisan support is "charter schools" – publicly funded schools open to every student through a lottery. These schools operate independently of the existing school district. Supporters of charter schools argue that if they work well and parents are satisfied with the education they provide, failing schools within the public system could improve by modeling themselves on the charter schools.

Unfortunately, tremendous inequality of educational opportunity in the United States persists, despite the fact that there is universal public schooling. Most education policy analysts argue that badly performing schools reflect the lack of economic opportunity of the communities they serve: schools in areas with low tax bases, where parents are chronically under-employed and where children lack the security to thrive because of crime or poor nutrition, simply do not have the financial and cultural resources to create a thriving educational environment.

These laws affecting education policy, and the laws governing family arrangements discussed above, elicit ambiguous feelings in American citizens about the proper role of the federal, state and local governments. Because each policy area directly touches individuals, families and communities in a very intimate way, there is a tendency for many Americans to want to keep control of these policies at the state level and if possible at the local level of cities, counties and towns. Yet, national policy makers in both political parties do not shy away from crafting laws in Congress and writing rules in the federal bureaucracy that will govern each of these policy areas. It is common for citizens to appeal to the federal government to shift local policies they do not like. And, members of both parties are perfectly willing to undermine local control of policies they do not support.

Cross-Cultural Dialogue 10: What to Learn in School

Michael : "I went to fantastic public schools growing up in Summit, New Jersey. I remember my fourth grade teacher, Mrs. Hansen, especially well. In her class we read good books, made dioramas of caves and buildings, and we learned geography and pre-algebra. I also remember my band teacher Mr. Andrews. By the time I was 11 years old, I had learned how to play the saxophone pretty well, and I played saxophone all the way through the rest of my schooling years, even up through college – all because of my public school. While I played music, I also took my academic studies very seriously. Mr. Kaplow, my high school English literature teacher had the students keep journals, write short stories and memorize Chaucer's *Canterbury Tales*. In my science classes we dissected pig fetuses and did physics experiments on roller coasters at amusement parks. Finally, perhaps because Americans have a strong sports culture, I was drawn to playing some sport competitively, and so I played soccer for the high school team for four years. Looking back at it now, I am grateful for the opportunities I had to learn new things, and to try out music and sports. Now that I am a parent, though, I'm beginning to think about how to encourage my kids, and whether it is better to focus on one thing or to sample and try out many things, as I did growing up. What do you remember most about your schooling growing up, and how do parents in Japan think about educating their children?"

Taka : "There have been wonderful teachers in my memory as well. Mr. Kurokawa inspired me with his enthusiasm for scientific experiments. Ms. Aoyama taught me how to write long essays. They tried to spend extra time for me to advance my interests. However, overall, the Japanese education is a little different from

the American in terms of its attitude toward students. For this sabbatical from September 2011 to March 2013, I came to the United States with my sons. One of the most interesting things in the United States is summer school. As with many kids, my sons went to different summer camps every week to learn many different things. I think it is a good system for kids to figure out what they like to do. There is no such system in Japan. Japanese kids are more likely to learn one thing for a long time. There is the phrase, 'Slow but steady wins the race.' It is considered a virtue that kids put so much effort and patience to be a master of one thing. Maybe 'the frontier spirit' is still lingering in American culture, which encourages people to try new things. When people were not happy in one place, they moved to the west to build a new life there. From this historical experience, perhaps Americans tend to think that giving up is not necessarily a bad thing, and trying new things is a good thing."

CHAPTER 11

Economic Policy
経済政策

　連邦政府の経済との係わり合い方においては３つの主要なアプローチがある。第１にレッセフェールというアプローチである。それは政府の経済への介入は最小限に抑えるべきだとするものである。第２にジョン・メイナード・ケインズによって唱えられたアプローチである。それによると、経済を牽引するのは商品の消費であるから、政府は経済を発展させるためには需要を刺激する役割を果たすべきだとする。最後にサプライサイド経済学が唱えるアプローチである。それは、経済を牽引するのは消費ではなく生産であり、税制、金融政策、規制緩和などによってビジネスにより良い環境を提供することが政府の役割だとする。本章はこれらのアプローチがどのようにアメリカの経済政策の発展に影響を及ぼしたのかについて述べる。

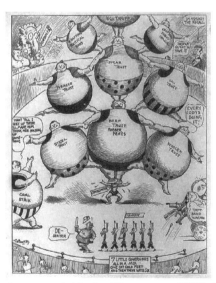

The Monopoly brothers supported by the little consumer (1912). This shows that big trusts had the power in the United States at that time, taking advantage of consumers. Courtesy of the U.S. Library of Congress.

There are three major approaches to how the federal government should deal with the economy. First, the laissez-faire approach claims that the government's involvement in the economy should be as little as possible. Second, the Keynesian approach suggests that the consumption of goods is the key to the health of the economy and the government should play a role in stimulating the demand side of the economy to generate economic growth. Lastly, the supply-side economics approach asserts that not consumption but production is the key and the government should create a better environment for business through tax and monetary policy, and reducing regulations. This chapter demonstrates how these three approaches affected the development of the economic policy of the United States.

The United States is now the economic super power in the world. But until the late 19th century, like Japan, it was one of the developing countries. After the 1860s, both Japan and the United States rapidly developed their economies. They did so in different ways, however. The Meiji government became intensively involved in the economy by making government-run companies and providing subsidies to private industries. It feared that Japan would have been colonized by western powers if it did not become a strong economic power. By contrast, the American economy originally grew with less governmental intervention. But, the role of the federal government has shifted and swung over time.

Although the United States has a strong tradition of a small federal government, there have always been political actors who have sought to increase its role in the economy. In 1800 Thomas Jefferson won the election and his idea of an agriculture-based economy diminished the role of the federal government. But in the twentieth century, the federal government began to play a much greater role in the economic downturns. By the 1980s, the conservative movement began to push again for a smaller federal government (at least in domestic policy), and that agenda intensified with Ronald Regan. More recently, President Barack Obama began to argue again that the federal government should play a role in achieving social justice.

Jefferson vs. Hamilton about the Future of the American Economy

In 1800, Alexander Hamilton, the first Secretary of the Treasury, and Thomas Jefferson, the first Secretary of State and later the third President, disagreed about what role industry would play in the American economy. Hamilton suggested that the United States should be based on commerce and manufacturers. On the other hand, Jefferson claimed that his country should be based on agriculture and independent farmers. These different opinions about the economy reflected their views of the federal government.

Along with President John Adams, Hamilton was in the Federalist Party, which supported the idea of a bigger federal government.[1] He argued that the federal government should play a leading role to boost the economy and catch up with European countries. His idea was more similar to what the Meiji bureaucrats had in their minds, in which the central government would invest in the start-up of key industries. Jefferson, on the other hand, led the Democratic Republican Party, which advocated a smaller federal government by interpreting the Constitution more narrowly. Jefferson was worried that federal support for financial and banking interests in the Northeast would lead to a government of wealthy elites who would create a large debtor class, and who in the process would undermine American self-reliance and the people's freedom.

Jefferson's election over Adams as the third president shaped the course of American economic development: the federal government would

---

[1] The supporters of the Federalist Party should not be confused with the authors of the Federalist Papers. The Federalist Party emerged after the Constitution was enacted to ask for the bigger federal government, and the Democratic Republican Party emerged as a counter force. James Madison, who was one of the authors of the Federalist Papers with Hamilton, later joined in the Republican-Democratic Party with Thomas Jefferson.

remain small, though it would promote expansion of an agriculture-based economy. This idea was realized in the western territories that Jefferson added to the nation with the Louisiana Purchase, where independent farmers cultivated the land. But in the mid-nineteenth century the industrial revolution came from Britain to the United States, and Jefferson's image of the nation, which had been carried through by his successors in the Democratic Party, and especially through Andrew Jackson, had to be revised.

The American Industrial Revolution

The American industrial revolution was different from comparable revolutions in European countries. In the eighteenth century, under the idea of mercantilism, the governments in major European countries began to protect their domestic industry, take control over international trade, expand their colonies, and increase the wealth of their countries. Although the British government had less power in the economic development than France and Spain, this top-down economic approach ushered European countries into the industrial revolution in the nineteenth century.

Japan also adopted the top-down approach to develop its industry. When the Meiji government was established, its priority was to protect the nation against the western countries through military and economic strength. Under the slogan, "rich country, strong economy *(Fukoku Kyohei)*," the government made government-managed enterprises to advance this industrialization. The Steel Manufacturing in Yawata was an example. Because the government saw the steel industry as a key to industrialization of Japan, it made investments to get the industry going in Yawata and then sold it to the private company.

The United States, on the other hand, experienced a different industrialization process that happened from the bottom-up, with little management from the central government. The impetus for the industrialization came to the United States with the Embargo Act of 1807 that prohibited trade with Britain and France and which led to the War of 1812 against

Britain. Without importing goods from these countries, the United States had to develop its own manufactures and to become more economically independent. But the federal government did not radically step into the economy under the presidency of James Madison, who shared with his ally Thomas Jefferson the same idea of small government. The manufactures began to develop, particularly on the east coast, without much incentive from the federal government.

The Civil War led to another push for industrialization of the economy. The governments of the Union and the Confederacy advanced technologies that the industrial revolution brought. In particular, both developed the transportation, medicine, and weapons industries. The war not only caused further industrialization, but also demonstrated that industrial strength was an important factor in making a country strong enough to win the war. The Union's victory was attributed to its higher degree of capitalist development and industrialization than was present in the Confederacy, which was based on slavery and an agricultural economy.

After the war, industrialization continued. In a sense, Hamilton's image of the American economy was realized, but the economic transformation was not lead by a strong national government, as it was in the cases of Japan and in Europe. The federal government still played a limited but important role in the economy by preparing infrastructure to facilitate interstate transportation and setting tariffs to protect American manufacturing. The federal government was based on the theory of laissez-faire that the government's involvement in the economy should be as little as possible. However, because of the federal system, states had plenty of authority to manage their economies as they saw fit, and many of the Northern state governments, including New York, did make large investments in infrastructure and education.

The Rise of Monopoly and the Federal Government

Further economic changes and the growth of large businesses in many of the states that began to move their business across state lines

The commercial club of Washington, by J.S. Pughe (1905). This shows that in the Senate Finance Committee Nelson Aldrich played a dominant role (in the throne) with his friends, like John Rockefeller (right bottom corner), for business interests. A man kneeling down in front of the King is Theodore Roosevelt. Courtesy of the U.S. Library of Congress.

caused problems that the federal government had to deal with. Monopolies appeared and the wealth was concentrated into a few dominant companies, such as John Rockefeller's Standard Oil Company and Andrew Carnegie's Steel Company. By the late 1890s, a Populist Party had formed which criticized how these companies reduced competition and hurt consumers, and how banks in the Northeast controlled the money supply in a way that hurt debtors. In 1901, William McKinley (Republican) became the president, but he followed the norm of allowing the states to deal with the problem if they saw fit, and keeping the federal government out of commerce. But a turning point came when McKinley was assassinated and Vice President Theodore Roosevelt succeeded to the presidency.

Theodore Roosevelt believed that fair competition and healthy capitalism had to be restored by regulating the monopolies – which at the time were called "trusts." His administration brought lawsuits against big companies that included the Standard Oil Company, and it won many of them. Standard Oil Company, as a result, was broken into smaller companies, which later became Exxon, Mobile, Chevron, Amoco and others. The next two presidents, William Taft (Republican) and Woodrow Wilson (Democrat), basically followed Roosevelt's anti-trust policy. But the federal government's involvement in the economy was still limited, only intervening when companies become much too large.

While America's entry into World War I led the federal government to expand its power in the economy to facilitate the war mobilization, the end of the war brought the sentiment of a "return to normalcy" including a desire for a federal government that would be less active in the economy and less visible in the lives of American citizens. The 1920s was an era of economic prosperity for the United States. By that time, a revolutionary production process had been invented. Henry Ford's new assembly line made the production of cars more efficient and less expensive. Whereas cars had been individually crafted by skilled workers, Ford's new assembly line allowed cars to move on a conveyer belt so that less skilled workers stood in the same place to do the same task again and again. Ford's idea inspired other industries and many products now became less expensive and available to the middle class.

As the economy boomed in the 1920s, the stock market and real estate values skyrocketed. The economic development took place without the federal government's support. Three Republican presidents – Calvin Coolidge, Warren Harding, and Herbert Hoover – followed the traditional view that the federal government should play a limited role, based on the idea of laissez-faire. It appeared that the American way was the best way to build the economy and generate national prosperity. However, the crash of the New York stock market in September 1929 showed that this view was wrong.

The Great Depression and the Federal Government

The Great Depression was an unprecedented economic downturn. Nobody was sure how to deal with it. Initially, President Hoover responded by encouraging the American people to give their money to charity, making financial arrangements to keep businesses running, and creating some public work projects, including the Hoover Dam. But he believed in the need to have balanced budgets and in the idea of "rugged individualism." He expected Americans citizens to pull themselves out of dire circumstances without significant government assistance. As a result, his measures were too little to be effective. Franklin D. Roosevelt (FDR), a Democrat, was elected in 1932 with new ideas about the government's role in the economy.

One of the first things Roosevelt did was to declare a bank moratorium in order to calm people's panic and stop them from withdrawing their saving from their banks. The National Industry Recovery Act was enacted to regulate industry and create public projects to increase employment, and the Agricultural Adjustment Act was established to subsidize farmers to adjust their production. The federal government also directly intervened in the economy by creating the Tennessee Valley Authority which was the largest government-managed enterprise to date. Many bridges and damns and man-made reservoirs in the United States today date back to FDR's response to the Great Depression. These economic policies were called "New Deal" programs.

This was the period when the Democratic Party clearly defined its stance toward the economy. Roosevelt's New Deal programs were based on the Keynesian approach: the federal government should help stimulate the demand side of the economy. It did this through massive expenditures on public works projects and new federal programs mentioned above, and discussed more in the next chapter. By employing people or providing them directly with income assistance, American consumers would have more money to spend on the economy, which would lead to growth.

During World War II, as during the previous world war, the federal government got involved in the economy to make the war mobilization more efficient. After the war, a sentiment of returning to normalcy again prevailed, with many Americans desiring again to see a reduced role of the federal government. But the government's role in the economy never got back to the more limited role it had played during the pre-1932 period. When the economy was down, the federal government was expected to produce measures to stimulate the economy. The New Deal economic policy continued under Dwight D. Eisenhower (Republican), John F. Kennedy (Democrat), and Lyndon B. Johnson (Democrat).

The federal government also played a leading role in investing in the development of science and technology. For example, the government expanded its funding to the National Institutes of Health (NIH) for medical research and to the National Aeronautics and Space Administration (NASA) for aeronautics and aerospace research. The federal government's investment in the armed forces, furthermore, has impacted technological developments. Many technological innovations from the government investments have been transferred to the private industries, including the launching of satellites into space, personal computers, and much later on, the internet.

But in the late 1960s, elected officials in the federal government began to see cracks in public support for the New Deal scheme. First, the American economy faced new challenges from other countries. The American economy boomed in the 1950s because its allies in Europe and Asia needed to recover from the devastation caused by WWII. In the 1960s, however, Japan and West Germany emerged as rising economic powers. The United States could not maintain its dominant economic position in the world.

Second, the federal government lost its financial strength and the people's trust in the government. In the mid-1960s, as more and more young soldiers were sent to the battlefields, American involvement in the Vietnam War was bogged down, and the public became very opposed to the war. War expenditure shrank the size of the economic policy expenditure. An anti-war movement emerged to criticize the Johnson administration. Many Americans began demonstrating in the streets and in public spaces in Washington, D.C. to protest the war. Elites were perplexed by the social disorder, and unsure of how to respond.

Questioning the Federal Government's Role in the Economy

With the people frustrated by Johnson's handling of the war and feeling anxious about the changing position of the United States on the global stage, Richard Nixon (Republican) was elected in 1968. He was the first president since FDR to question the federal government's active role in the economy. Then the 1970s was a bad decade for the American economy. Japan and West Germany continued to threaten American economic dominance and other NICS (newly industrializing countries), such as South Korea and Taiwan, became competitors to the United States. Meanwhile, the American economy faced an unprecedented stagflation when the economic downturn and inflation took place at the same time. As Figure 11.1 shows, the strength of the American economy declined in comparison with the rest of the world.

In 1980 Ronald Reagan (Republican) was elected. He sent the message, "government is not the solution to our problem; government is the problem." Reagan believed that the federal government distorted economic markets and that paradoxically, its high tax rates reduced federal revenues, because they discouraged business growth. He adopted the idea of "supply-

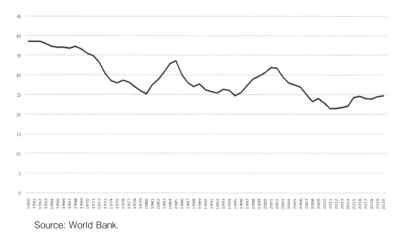

Source: World Bank.

Figure 11.1: American GDP in the World (%)

side economics." In this approach, the federal government should intervene in the economy not by stimulus policy but by creating a better environment for producers, by lowering tax rates and by deregulating constraints on businesses. Reagan also reduced the federal government's role in making and implementing federal projects. Reagan defined the Republican Party's stance toward economy policy, which continues into the present. The economic proposals of the Republican nominee for President in 2012, Mitt Romney, sounded very familiar to Reagan's proposals in 1980.

The American economy, however, did not see a dramatic improvement in economic conditions as a result of Reagan's policies. Moreover, lowering tax rates had the effect of decreasing revenues. Reagan's successor, George H. W. Bush (Republican) had to raise taxes to secure enough revenue to try to balance the federal budget. Many people were frustrated with the slow economic growth and the broken promise of Bush's: "Read my lips: no new taxes." When Bill Clinton ran for the president against Bush in 1992, he often used a phrase, "It's the economy, stupid!" Although Bush was very popular after the invasion of Iraq in March 1991, Clinton successfully shifted the public attention to the economy, and he was elected as the President.

What Clinton did in the area of economic policy was not really a clear departure from the preceding two conservative presidents. He took the "Third Way" approach, going between demand-side and supply-side policies. He never suggested a full return to the New Deal economic policy scheme in which the federal government plays the leading role to stimulate consumption. However, he did make investments in some industries, such as new information technologies, and he promoted technological advancement and new jobs. His priority was to achieve the balanced budget. He sought to make the federal government more modernized and efficient and if necessary he chose to discontinue programs. For example, with the Republican Congress he reformed the welfare program to reduce the financial burden on the federal government (see Chapter 12). The American economy seemed to be going well in Clinton's second term. But, the more fundamental change in the economy was taking place globally.

Globalization – the flow of human resources, products, and capital across national borders – has given all countries a new challenge. Jobs, especially those involving manual labor, move to countries with lower-wage workers. Headquarters of the companies move to countries with lower-tax rates. The governments try to lower taxes for big companies to stay at home, but this reduces their revenue and creates pressures to reduce spending on domestic economic and social policy. In the globalized economy, some say that all countries "race to the bottom." In advanced countries, this translates into fewer jobs for manual laborers and unskilled workers. When the economy is good, the structural problem does not come to the surface. But once a big recession happens, the mismatch between skills and available jobs, and the reduced revenues for government as a result of unemployment creates big problems. The unemployment rate does not easily improve and the government lacks the financial resources to boost the economy. This is exactly what countries experienced after the Great Recession of 2007, which began with the collapse of the bank, Lehman

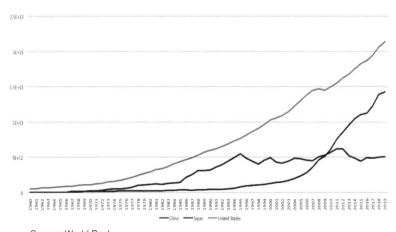

Source: World Bank.

Figure 11.2: GDP of Japan, China, and the United States (Current US $)

Brothers.

Economic globalization also makes it more difficult for the federal government to make effective economic policy by itself, since economies across the globe have become increasingly intertwined. The American economy is deeply connected with other countries. In particular, while China has recently had a significant economic development (Figure 11.2), its ties with the American economy have become deeper and deeper. Therefore, the American government has to think not only about how to compete with other economies, but also how to coexist with others.

The Power of Business in American Politics

Lastly, it should be noted that the power of business groups is strong in American politics for three reasons. First, because of the Constitutional framework, particularly federalism, the state governments become obstacles to the federal government's intervention in the economy. The state governments try to make better business environments by lowering taxes and giving subsidies to businesses. They do this to compete with other states to attract businesses to their state – just as nations do in the context of the global economy.

Second, there is a strong tradition in American politics of opposition to a federal role in regulating business. While this tradition is frequently challenged by populist arguments that the federal government needs to reduce the power of large corporations, generally speaking, Americans are wary of federal regulations of business. All Americans share the idea that the United States is a country of equal opportunity and that as long as everyone gets a "fair shot," as President Obama often says, individuals' efforts should be rewarded with personal and financial success. This idea of the "American Dream" is often translated into the argument that wealthy people deserve all of their wealth, and should be celebrated for their success, and not punished by high tax rates. Even when populist sentiments move Americans to challenge the power of the wealthy, they only ask that the wealthy contribute a little more, not that wealth inequality itself is a bad thing. No one wants to get rid of the idea of the American Dream, which is that their children will be better off than they are someday.

Third, in comparison to Europe, American labor power is weak. Labor unions are supposed to counter the power of business. The United States has a two party system and most labor unions support the Democratic Party. But because the Democratic Party includes many other interest groups, it cannot be a strong representative of labor unions. In addition, the labor unions are in effect "captured" by the Democratic Party – they could threaten to throw their support behind the Republican Party – but they are highly unlikely to do that since the Republican Party is openly hostile to them. So, while Democrats do respond to labor, labor has relatively weak leverage with Democratic officials. This is different from countries that have strong labor parties, which can have significant influence on national government.

Japan is an interesting case to add to this US-Europe comparison. Japan relies on a multi-party system, but for about fifty years after World War II, the power of the Liberal Democratic Party was so strong that the Socialist Party, which was backed by one of the largest labor unions, the General Council of Trade Unions of Japan (Sohyo in Japanese), had little political influence. Because of this history of party politics, the power of business has been strong. This is one of the reasons why social security expenditure in Japan is lower than it is in many European countries (see Figure 12.1 in the next chapter). In terms of the power of business, Japan and the United States are similar cases while they are different in terms of the power of the central government.

Cross-Cultural Dialogue 11: A Love Affair with Cars

Michael : "The American economy consumes about one quarter of total oil sales on the planet, and a big component of that consumption is the gasoline that goes into the cars Americans drive. So much of American life is "driven" by the car: beginning in the 1950s, sprawling suburbs sprang up around large cities because of huge public investments in roads and highways, which made it possible for Americans to live in cute little towns and commute by cars to go to work. Shopping malls with large parking lots also sprang up to serve customers who would drive five or ten miles to shop at them. The cars Americans used to drive were always made by American companies – Ford, Chevrolet and Chrysler. But now, Americans are as likely to buy cars from Toyota as they are to buy cars from Ford. The animosity Americans in the 1980s felt toward Japanese success is long gone. Now with so many successful Toyota plants in the United States, many Americans don't think twice about the national location of the corporate office. The Toyota Camry feels like an American car. The American love affairs with cars fascinates me because it tells us so much about American habits of consumption, the important role government plays in supporting economic choices, and the unpredictable consequences of globalization. What is the role of cars in Japan and how do the Japanese view their automobile companies and the Americans who buy so many of their products?"

Taka : "I have to confess that when I was a graduate student at Johns Hopkins, I drove a Buick Park Avenue, which was a huge American car. And now, I am driving a Chrysler Pacifica. As an American studies scholar, I have kind of decided that I drive American cars when I am in the United States. Some people think that

American cars are all bad. But at least from my experiences, it is not really true. But yes, they consume a lot of gas! And one more thing, Nanzan University is located in Nagoya, which is kind of the 'Japanese Detroit,' and home of the Toyota Automobile Industry. So there I feel much more strongly than I do in my hometown Fukui, about the importance of the car industry. And it has been one of the most important industries for Japan in terms of the domestic employment and international export. Also, your point about American habits of consumption is very interesting! For example, I can see while Japanese people still think Ichiro Suzuki is a Japanese player (yes, he is still a Japanese citizen), many Americans seem to think he is 'their' player. That shows that Americans embrace things not based on their origins. The example of Ichiro is just like what immigrants have been through. I do not think it works the same way in Japan. Even if Alex Rodrigues plays in Japan for a long time, and even if he were naturalized into a Japanese citizen, the Japanese people would never see him as 'one of them.'"

CHAPTER 12

Social Security and Welfare Policy
社会保障と福祉政策

　第11章で議論した経済政策に加え、社会保障を提供し国民の福祉の向上に寄与する政策のあり方は富の再分配を行うことから国家の経済に大きな影響を及ぼす。さらに、これらの政策は、国民がお互いをそして国家をどのような存在として見るのかにも左右する。それに含まれる政策分野は、失業、医療、貧困、高齢者対策など多岐にわたっている。国家はそれぞれ異なった社会政策を採用している。本章はアメリカの社会政策がどのように発展したのか、そして現在どのような形になっているのについて述べる。

President Obama (left) and Health and Human Service Secretary Kathleen Sebelius (right) visited a Philadelphia area Head Start Center which supports low income children. Source: www.hhs.gov.

In addition to economic policy, discussed in the last chapter, policy to provide social security and promote the general welfare has a big impact on the national economy by redistributing wealth. Furthermore, it affects how the people see each other and their nation. It could include a wide range of policy areas, such as unemployment, health care, poverty, and old-age programs. Each country has a different set of social policies. This chapter shows the development of social policy in the United States and what it looks like today.

In March 2010, the Obama Administration celebrated the passage of the Patient Protection and Affordable Act. With this law, the federal government took a bold step to secure the enrollment of all Americans in health insurance. Obama believed in universal health care, or the idea that the government has a moral responsibility to ensure that all Americans have access to health care. But the opponents of the health care reform continued even after the passage to try to repeal the legislation. They argued that the health care reform would result in giving too much power to the federal government, against the spirit of the Founding Fathers.

To many Japanese people, this political struggle to introduce universal health insurance looked strange. Japanese people have been enjoying the benefit of a universal health insurance system since 1961, and they tend to think it natural that the central government takes responsibility for guaranteeing health care for all citizens. Unlike many Americans, they do not give a serious consideration to the problems that arise from government funding for expensive programs like health care. They also are less likely to think that social security and welfare programs could be a threat to their freedoms.[1] To them, social security policy and welfare policy exist

---

[1] When ordinary Americans hear the term "social security," they tend to think it refers to the old-aged pension because the public old-aged pension program (also survivors and disabilities) is named "Social Security."

to protect them from the insecurity of living in a capitalist economy. But many Americans, particularly economic conservatives, think that those policies limit their freedom to seek their own happiness. One major argument against Obama's health care reform was that the new law would threaten the people's freedom to decide whether they would join a health insurance plan or not, and that it would limit what kind of health care they could receive.

The Limited American Welfare State

The United States has lower public expenditures on social policy than Japan and other major European countries. In 2008, the public expenditure on social policy, including old-age, health, unemployment, housing and other social policy areas, occupied 16.8% of GDP in the United States while it was 20.0% in Japan, 21.5% in England, 25.2% in Germany, and 28.6% in France. The American federal government plays a smaller role in making a safety net for the people.

Scholars have discussed why the United States lagged behind other advanced countries in terms of the development of social policy. There are three major factors – constitutional, cultural, and political.

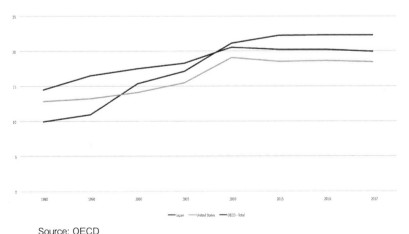

Source: OECD

Figure 12: Public Social Spending in Japan, the United States, and EU 21 (% of GDP)

The U.S. Constitution, as discussed in Chapter 2, makes it difficult for the federal government to make large-scale social policy. Federalism and the concept of the enumerated powers constrain what the federal government can do (see Chapter 4). The Constitution does not specifically stipulate that the federal government has the right to get involved in old-age pensions, health insurance, unemployment insurance, and so on. It does not guarantee overall responsibility of the federal government in securing people's well being, either. It merely says that the purpose of the Constitution is "to promote the general welfare." This is very different from the Japanese Constitution in which Article 25 does guarantee the central government's responsibility for securing the people's right "to maintain the minimum standards of wholesome and cultured living."

Development of social policy has also been slow and difficult because the separation of powers system results in less coordination between Congress and the President. The rivalry between the two branches, especially when different parties control each branch, makes the establishment of major social policy less likely. In addition, the Supreme Court has played a role in blocking the radical expansion of the federal government's power by declaring major acts of social policy legislation unconstitutional.

American political culture has also slowed down the development of social policy. The opponents of social policy effectively use the idea of freedom to oppose expansion of the size of government. Any increase in government is described by these opponents as a threat to the freedom of citizens. They claim that freedom from government interference in private choices is what the United States is based on. There is no such cultural discourse in Japan. In the United States, this culture of liberty has been an obstacle to the federal government's attempts to intervene in the private sphere. In addition, Americans are more allergic to the idea of socialism than the Japanese people are. To mobilize public sentiment against government support for health care, for example, the opponents of universal health insurance have often claimed that it is socialized medicine.

Lastly, political context has shaped the lagged development of social policy in the United States. One aspect should be focused on here: the political weakness of organized labor. As discussed in Chapter 11, organized labor in the United States has been politically less powerful than its counterparts in the major European countries. Political scientists have shown that where labor unions are politically powerful, they have more effectively pushed the government to expand the social safety net for them. But, American labor unions are politically weak because they cannot represent their interests by creating their own political party under the American two-party system. To make it worse, organized labor relies mostly on the Democratic Party while business groups have strong political influence on both parties. Racial and ethnic division also prevents organized labor from solidifying into a unified front.

These factors make expenditures on American social policy quantitatively smaller than they are in European countries. But they also make social policy qualitatively different in several ways. First, the idea of self-help has strongly and consistently affected social policy making in the United States more so than in other countries. Whether the targeted group is needy or not is always under scrutiny. Welfare dependency not only creates a financial burden for the government; it also goes against the ideas of the Founding Fathers. Because of this respect for self-help, public spending on people who are capable but who fail to help themselves – who scholars have referred to as the "undeserving poor" – have been politically unpopular in the United States.

However, two kinds of public programs are more widely supported by the American public. The first are programs that support people who, earlier in their lives, contributed taxes into the system. Old-aged pension programs in the United States and Japan are good examples of contributory programs. They are more popular than cash assistance programs for people with low incomes. In the contributory programs, people start to pay contributions in their early age so that they accumulate benefits for their retirement life. These programs differ from non-contributory programs in which people receive benefits they did not contribute to, with the government bearing the cost.

The second are non-contributory programs that protect the "deserving poor" – that is, people whose poverty arises through no fault of their own, or stems from a social position that is respected. Examples of programs for the "deserving poor" include income assistance for mothers, children, disabled people and wounded veterans. Able-bodied men and able-bodied women without children are considered less needy than single women with children, or disabled people who cannot work. Although cash assistance for the poor is generally unpopular, the welfare programs that do exist for people with low incomes, including public health insurance for the poor, have targeted mainly mothers and children, who society views as deserving the aid. Political scientist Theda Skocpol demonstrates that public assistance to mothers and children was more generous in the United States than in Britain in the 1930s when overall social policy expenditure was larger in Britain.

Another unusual characteristic of American social policy is that the private sector plays a great role. The private sector not only gets involved in public programs as insurers and service providers but the goods provided by private business also become substitutes for public programs. For example, while private health insurance only supplements public insurance in Japan, private health insurance is the core of the American health care system. Preferential tax policy is also a tool that the federal government uses to make the private services more accessible to the people. Political scientist Christopher Howard calls this government's indirect expenditure the "hidden welfare state," and argues that the hidden American welfare state is larger than its more visible European counterparts.

The Expansion of Social Security and Welfare Policy

Given these constitutional, cultural, and political constraints, American social policy began to develop in the early 20th century. In face of the deterioration of working conditions particularly in big cities, state governments started to establish workers' compensation laws which allowed workers to receive payments for their occupation-connected diseases and injuries. The Progressive movement was the first major attempt to push not only state governments but also the federal government to get involved in social policy. Progressives formed the American Association for Labor Legislation to gather reform-minded intellectuals and push for the expansion of social policy.

Building on the successes of Progressive reformers in some states such as New York and Wisconsin, reformers at the national level helped the federal government to pass child labor laws. The Keating-Owen Act of 1916 aimed to punish factories, mines, and other facilities that did not meet the federal government's child labor regulation. Although the Supreme Court declared the law unconstitutional in 1918, many states began to plan their own regulations because of its passage. By 1929, all states prohibited business from hiring children under the age of fourteen.

The Progressive reformers also tried to introduce state-level public health insurance for workers. Although their dream for public health insurance was never realized, a health care program for mothers and children passed in Congress as the Sheppard-Towner Maternity and Infancy Protection Act of 1921. The law provided 50-50 matching funds to states for creating health care clinics for women and infants.

The Progressive movement dispersed during the mid-1920s. With the "return to normalcy" after World War I and the postwar economic development that improved the conditions of many workers, Progressive reformers had trouble mobilizing public support for their ideas about government, and the movement lost some legitimacy. The Sheppard-Towner Act was also discontinued during this conservative period. But soon the reformers found an opportunity to revive their movement when the Great Depression occurred.

With the crisis of massive unemployment and a lack of consumption

in the economy, the expansion of social poli-
cy became part of the "New Deal," discussed briefly in Chapter 11. The New
Deal aimed at making 3 R's: Relief,
Recovery, and Reform. President Franklin
D. Roosevelt, a Progressive who had
worked in Woodrow Wilson's administration, led Congress to enact the Social
Security Act of 1935. Among many programs, two major contributory programs
were included: the Federal Old-Age,
Survivors, and Disability Insurance and the
Unemployment Insurance. The Aid to
Families with Dependent Children was also
included to provide financial support to

Franklin Roosevelt, who expanded
social security and welfare programs,
was in a wheelchair after he had a
high fever and paralyzed his legs at
the age of 39. Courtesy of the FDR
Presidential Library and Museum.

children with single parents or low-income families. It was a non-contributory program that targeted mainly mothers and children – two deserving cat-
egories of the poor.

Although Roosevelt achieved these unprecedented policy developments, there was one major policy he could not include in the Social
Security Act. It was the establishment of a public health insurance program
for workers. When the American Medical Association and its allies knew
that the Roosevelt administration was studying health insurance, they conducted a campaign to oppose any policy development in health insurance.
They labeled public health insurance as socialized medicine. Roosevelt gave
up including health insurance as part of the overall package of social policy
because he feared that opposition to health insurance could ruin the entire
social security legislation.

Even without health insurance, the New Deal set a new policy
scheme that could not be reversed easily. The end of World War II again
caused the sentiment of "a return to normalcy," but normalcy did not mean

the same thing as it had meant after World War I. Right after the war, Harry S. Truman presented a 21 point program to suggest that the federal government play a stronger role in economic and social policy. It was based on what Roosevelt proposed in 1944 for the postwar reconstruction period.

The Republican President, Dwight D. Eisenhower, was elected in 1952. Although Republicans were less friendly to a bigger governmental role in social policy, Eisenhower and the public continued to support the basic concept of the New Deal, and the Democratic Party remained the majority party in both houses. But limitations on reform came not only from Republicans but also from conservative Democrats, mainly ones from the southern states. The Southern Democrats opposed some measures like universal health insurance because they were concerned that federal programs would interfere with their states' rights to decide intra-state affairs, including the system of legal racial segregation. Moreover, the economic boom in the 1950s made it harder for the federal government to justify the radical expansion of its power in social policy.

But in the 1960s, reformers saw an opportunity to push for the pending issues. When the Democrat John F. Kennedy was elected President, he brought young energy to the White House. Like FDR's administration before his, Kennedy's administration included enthusiastic social scientists such as Daniel Patrick Moynihan, who later became a Senator from New York, who engaged in the planning of social problems. In the early 1960s, the poverty problem was revisited because studies found that poverty remained even after the economic boom in the 1950s. In 1962, Michael Harrington's book, *The Other America*, articulated that the culture of poverty binds people in poverty and that the culture of poverty was not attributed to individuals but to the social structure. The administration gradually shifted its priority from social policy reform to broader social reform.

The assassination of Kennedy intensified the enthusiasm for social reform. Soon after he was sworn into office, Lyndon B. Johnson declared a

"War on Poverty" to combat the persistent poverty problem. A new policy scheme was introduced in the newly created Economic Opportunity Act. The main idea behind the act was that it is critical to empower the poor rather than to merely offer them "handouts."

Johnson called for a larger domestic policy package, named the "Great Society" program. The grand vision of the Great Society was to end racial discrimination and poverty. Johnson's goal was to build on the progressive changes that FDR began thirty years earlier. In addition to the economic security Roosevelt had sought, Johnson also built upon the advances made by Truman toward civil rights and political equality for American minorities, and especially African Americans. The Civil Rights Act of 1964 and the Voting Act of 1965 sought to bring an end to legal racial discrimination, which was still common in many parts of the country, and especially the South. The Aid to Families with Dependent Children was expanded. The Head Start program was established to help children in poor families to have education before they entered kindergarten. Many job-training programs were created to support unemployed people.

Johnson achieved what presidents going back to progressives at the turn of the twentieth century like Teddy Roosevelt could not: health care reform. But he could not achieve universal health insurance, either. By the 1960s, the coverage by private health insurance plans offered by employers had increased, but it was obvious that many Americans did not have access to these plans. Some reformers advocated that the United States should adopt a single-payer national health insurance system. But this plan was not realized because of opposition

President Johnson signs Medicare. Former President Harry Truman is sitting next to him. Courtesy of the Harry S. Truman Library and Museum.

from the American Medical Association and its allies. Instead, in 1965, two public health insurance programs were formed. Medicaid was a means-tested program for individuals and families living with low incomes, and Medicare was established as a universal program for all people over the age of 65 and for younger people with disabilities. This was a more moderate achievement than what some radical reformers had wished for, but the Great Society nevertheless expanded the size and power of the federal government.

The Retrenchment of Social Security and Welfare Policy

In 1968, Republican candidate Richard Nixon was elected as the President. He expanded many programs, such as the Old-Age Pension, Food Stamp, and cash assistance programs for the elderly, the disabled and the poor. But he amended the Great Society program in key ways. First, he withdrew from Johnson's policy scheme in which the federal government should empower the poor by letting them participate in the policy process. Nixon concluded that the policy scheme did not work as intended and instead caused social and political confusion. Furthermore, he paid special attention to assisting the working poor. The working poor are those whose incomes placed them just above the poverty line, but who still have a hard time making a living. While the Johnson administration's policy had focused more on the non-working poor, who many thought were undeserving of public support, Nixon's shift toward supporting the working poor had much broader public support.

While Nixon sought to modify the Great Society program, Ronald Reagan conducted an all-out war against the trend of bigger and bigger government set in motion by the New Deal and Great Society programs. Reagan's speech in 1964 to support the presidential candidate Barry Goldwater made him famous. He said, "This is the issue of this election: Whether we believe in our capacity for self-government or whether we abandon the American revolution and confess that a little intellectual elite in a far-distant capitol can plan our lives for us better than we can plan them ourselves." He won the presidential election in 1980 by ringing the death knell to the idea of big government and large social policy.

While Regan cut taxes, he also reduced the budget for social policy. He was an enthusiastic believer in the free market economy. He attributed the stagnated economy to the legacy of the federal government's excessive power. He sought to decrease the power of the federal government by reducing the number of federal regulations on business and on the states, and reducing its large expenditures (except in the foreign policy area, as discussed in the next chapter). Reagan emphasized that the federal government's focus should be to help only the neediest Americans, those at the bottom of the social class ladder.

In 1994, Reagan's vision for welfare reform was realized by a big policy change during the presidential administration of Bill Clinton, a southern Democrat from Arkansas. The Personal Responsibility and Work Opportunity Reconciliation Act of 1996 (PRWORA) replaced AFDC with the Temporary Assistance for Needy Families (TANF). The nature of the cash assistance programs to poor families changed. Unlike the AFDC, the TANF is not an entitlement program. With AFDC, the federal government guaranteed benefits to people whose income and assets were below the eligibility level. But the federal government does not guarantee these benefits for TANF. Instead, it gives block grants to the state governments where officials at the state level have more discretion to determine who is eligible for the aid. Moreover, the shift from AFDC to TANF reflected a shift "from welfare to workfare." By stipulating that people can benefit from the TANF program for a total of only five years, the federal government emphasized not social but individual responsibility as a basis for moving people out of poverty.

The PROWORA was passed by a Republican Congress. But it is important to emphasize that the Democratic President Bill Clinton cooperated with them. Serious reconsideration about the New Deal social policy now came not only from the Republican Party but also from the Democratic

Party. President Clinton concluded that the United States needed significant modification to the New Deal social policy to meet the changing economic environment.

In that new environment, the economy was not growing much, low wage jobs were going abroad, and big companies moved their corporate headquarters to countries that offered lower tax rates. In the face of that economic climate, and in order to keep the budget relatively balanced, Clinton kept taxes higher on wealthy Americans. But the economy was unstable, and there was a recession early in the term of George W. Bush. In response, Bush cut taxes for all Americans. Today, the federal government has a hard time increasing its revenues, and national budget deficits occur regularly each year. As a result, while more people in the middle class are exposed to the possibility of poverty, the government has less money to assist those who are in need. Particularly, the federal government faced a serious financial crisis after the Lehman shock in 2007.

The Birth of a New Model?

President Obama took office in the worst economic downturn the United States had faced since the Great Depression. In this difficult time, the Obama Administration proposed health care reform, so-called Obamacare. His plan did not create a new national program to cover all the people; rather, it utilized the existing private health insurance markets to try to increase coverage. In order to increase access the to private plans, the new law required people who did not already have health care from their employer or from the government to purchase it, or to pay a penalty. Through this penalty and by raising other revenues to make the system work, the federal government significantly expanded its power.

The question was whether this health care reform would lead to a revival of the New Deal social policy. The opponents have continued their campaign to repeal it. They often argued that it went against the United States' founding principles because it resulted in a radical expansion of the federal government in size and power. On the other hand, the Obama

Administration insisted that the health care reform was not a typical idea of the big federal government. Rather it was a combination of progressive and conservative ideas by maintaining private actors as the main health insurance providers.

The political battle was brought into the court. In June 2012, the Supreme Court upheld a key provision of Obamacare. The majority opinion said, "Congress passed the Affordable Care Act [Obamacare] to improve health insurance markets, not to destroy them." Then in few months, President Obama was reelected. After that, Republican Speaker of House Johns Boehner said, "Obamacare is the law of the land."

However, Republicans continued to attack Obamacare. They tried many times to repeal it. Then they had Donald Trump elected in 2016. But they never succeeded to abolish Obamacare. That was because Obamacare expanded the health insurance coverage to many people and the public began to see it more positively. As the health care cost increased, more people appreciated the federal government's intervention.

Then the COVID-19 pandemic came to the United States in the early 2020. The United States soon saw the highest number of confirmed cases and deaths. Scholars argued it was because of health insurance problems. Obamacare's fatal defect was that it was not universal health insurance. In 2018, 8.5% of the population was uninsured. There were many people who did not have health insurance and enrolled in cheap plan which required them pay a lot of out-of-pocket expenses. They hesitated to go COVID-19 testing and see doctors.

COVID-19 made the problems of health access visible. The gap in health access was overlapped with the income gap. While many high-income people could work remotely, many poor people were employed in service occupations and more often exposed to the virus. Donald Trump decided to invest in the vaccine development, but he did not promise to improve the social security system.

In the 2020 presidential election, the people chose Joe Biden. He pledged to engage in the improvement of Obamacare and other social security programs, and elimination of racial disparities. What the Biden administration can do affects the future course of American social policy.

Cross-Cultural Dialogue 12: Sick Health Care Systems

Michael : "I generally support the overall goal of the Patient Protection and Affordable Care Act, and I get frustrated by conservative arguments that it is socialist, or amounts to a government take-over of health care. The American health care system is sick: millions of Americans lack affordable health care coverage, though the number of Americans without health insurance will decline because of Obama's new health care law. The costs of health care are tremendously high, primarily because the system is inefficient, and there are a hundred little things that make costs go up. I'll just name two. First, people who do not have health insurance will still get health care in emergency rooms if the really need it, which is very expensive. Second, the care that doctors provide is expensive because they prescribe more tests and procedures than patients need because they worry about being sued if a patient's sickness goes undetected. The new health care law tries to bring down these costs by bringing all Americans into the private market system. That's good because more people have coverage, but bad because the system itself sick! Unfortunately, the controversy over this law is filled with misinformation on both sides, which is very frustrating. How do the Japanese view their health care system?   What do they make of the American version, and would they warn Americans about the dangers of more government control?"

Taka : "First of all, the Japanese health care system is not healthy, either. In August 2006, a woman who had a brain hemorrhage in Nara Prefecture died in the ambulance after being rejected by nineteen hospitals. This kind of event happens again and again. That is largely because the national health insurance fee schedule is too

low for many hospitals to have enough staffs in obstetrics, gynecology, and pediatrics sections. Many doctors employed by hospitals, as a result, have suffered from overwork and some have committed suicide. Moreover, many patients cannot have sufficient care in busy hospitals. But the Japanese health care system has also demonstrated a good performance. Japanese people now live longest in the world. I think that the government should guarantee the minimum health care coverage to the people. But the people and the government should together decide what the minimum coverage should be and how they pay for the system. I believe that the national medical association is the key player. Both the Japan Medical Association and the American Medical Association seem to be considered by the public to protect only the interests of doctors. They should be thinking more seriously about advocating patients' interests because they are the ones seeing patients everyday. Among many social programs, health care policy deals more directly with people's concept of life and death, and it should reflect how the people pursue their happiness."

CHAPTER 13

Foreign Policy
外交政策

アメリカの外交政策には、孤立主義と国際主義という二つの考え方が存在する。前者は、アメリカはその他の世界とは政治的に関わるべきではないとする。そして後者は、アメリカは国際政治に積極的に関与し協力すべきであるという考え方である。日本の徳川時代には孤立主義的な政策を採っていた。しかし徳川時代の終焉とともにその政策は終わった。他方、アメリカの孤立主義の伝統はすべて消えたわけではない。それは未だにアメリカが国際社会でどのように振る舞うべきかを考える時に影響を与えるものである。本章は、アメリカ外交政策に影響を与えた政治システム、アイディア、そして歴史的出来事について述べる。

Keep off! The Monroe Doctrine must be respected (1896). This picture shows that an American soldier is claiming to Europeans that they have no rights to intervene in affairs in the American continent. Courtesy of the U.S. Library of Congress.

There are two schools of thought about American foreign policy: isolationism and internationalism. The former suggests that the United States should not deal with the politics of the rest of the world. The latter claims that the United States should get actively engaged in international politics and cooperation. Japan had its own isolationism policy in the Tokugawa Era. But it disappeared with the collapse of the Shogunate. American isolationism, by contrast, has not completely gone out; it is still affecting how the United States behaves in the international community. This chapter describes the political system, ideas, and historical events that shaped American foreign policy.

"Who is the most powerful person in the world?" When Japanese people are asked this question, many people answer, "the American President." But remember that we have talked about how the fragmented American political system prevents one person or institution from having too much power, and the President is no exception. Political scientist Richard Neustadt describes the President as a soft leader who cannot force others to do things they do not like but can persuade them to take some course of action. Do Japanese people see an illusion of the powerful president? Not exactly: the extent of his influence depends on the policy area. The President can cast more influence in foreign policy than in domestic policy. Japanese people do not often see how the American President performs in domestic politics, but they often witness how the President represents the voice of the United States in international politics.

The President as Commander in Chief

Article 2 Section 2 of the Constitution reads, "The President shall be commander in chief of the Army and Navy of the United States." The President is responsible for the American military involvements in the world, including the use of military force abroad, though not including a declaration of war with another nation, which is formally delegated to

Congress. The Constitution also empowers the President to play a leading role in diplomacy and making treaties. Because the details about the war operation and diplomacy are often invisible to the public, the President will make decisions only with his close advisers. It can be concluded that he has more power and discretion in foreign policy than in domestic policy.

But the Constitution does not grant the President full authority in foreign policy. Congress has the authority to formally declare war, to give disapproval of President-led military actions that occur without a declaration of war,[1] and to control the war-related budget and affect the course of war by the funding process. It also has the power to reject treaties the President makes. Thus, the checks and balances system also applies to foreign policy as it does to domestic policy, but to a more limited extent. With these institutional constraints, the Presidents have tried to shape foreign policy.

The Tradition of Isolationism

There are two basic questions about American foreign policy. The first is whether the United States should interact with the rest of the world. The second question is, "*if* the United States has to deal with other countries, then how should it do so?" One idea was that the United States should cooperate with other countries to deal with problems. The other was that it should act in a unilateral way to achieve its own interests. During the first half of American history, Americans primarily debated the first question. One vision was that the United States should get involved in the politics of Europe. The other was that it should have distance from European politics.

In 1796, at the end of his two terms as the first President of the United States, George Washington articulated a vision of American foreign policy in his "Farewell Address." After seeing the nation's politics during its first eight years, Washington feared that the United States would break

---

[1] This is stipulated in the War Powers Resolution of 1973. But it has been neglected by the Presidents in many cases, such as Clinton's bombing in Kosovo in 1999.

up because of the conflicts between two political parties: the Federalist Party and the Democratic-Republican Party. In his address, he stressed that the United States should refocus on its founding principles and overcome the internal conflicts.

To unite the country, Washington suggested that the United States should not get involved in European politics. There was a fierce power struggle in Europe, especially between Britain and France. Washington worried that the Federalist Party's sympathy for Britain and the Democratic-Republican Party's sympathy for France would divide the United States apart. He noted in the address, "It is our true policy to steer clear of permanent alliances with any portion of the foreign world ... ." He did not deny short-term alliances for national emergencies, and neither did he deny the economic relationship with European countries. But Washington emphasized that the United States should avoid its permanent military engagement with particular countries and break off unrestrained interaction with all nations.

In 1823, President James Monroe reconfirmed what Washington claimed, in a policy that came to be called the Monroe Doctrine. By that time, many Latin American colonies of Spain and Portugal either had become independent nations, or were trying to achieve independence. He contrasted the revolutionary spirit in the New World on the American continents with the monarchical and imperial rivalries of the Old World across the Atlantic Ocean. Monroe suggested that the United States would not deal with European politics and that European countries should not get involved in the United States, or with the newly independent Latin American countries. Monroe stated that "the American continents, by the free and independent condition which they have assumed and maintain, are henceforth not to be considered as subjects for future colonization by any European powers."

The Monroe Doctrine – prohibiting military alliances but allowing commercial interaction – was possible under that particular time and geography. First, the Atlantic Ocean separated Britain and the United States by about 3,000 miles (4,828 kilometers) and it took more than two months for the contemporary ships to travel that distance. Second, European countries were too busy with their power struggles in the European continent to deal with the New World. These conditions made it possible for the United States to maintain the Monroe Doctrine throughout the nineteenth century.

Some Japanese people might see a parallel between the United States' isolationist policy and the Japanese *Sakoku* policy. In 1639, the Tokugawa Shogunate began its isolationism in fear of foreign countries, such as Spain and Portugal that were competing to expand their imperial power outside Europe. The Shoguante also feared that through communication with western nations, Christianity would spread and break down the social structure that the Tokugawa Shogunate relied on. Christianity's claim that all people are equal under God was a serious challenge to the social and political hierarchy in Japan. This Japanese isolationist policy continued about two hundred years. It was made possible largely because European nations were busy fighting each other and Japan was geographically detached from Europe.

However, there is an important difference between the two isolationist policies. While American isolationism was justified to preserve the founding principles – small central authority – in contrast to the Old World, the Japanese isolationism was to strengthen the authority of the Tokugawa Shogunate. Therefore, the tradition of Japanese isolationism ended with the collapse of the Tokugawa Shogunate. But American isolationism continued to affect American foreign policy even after the United States actually engaged in European politics.

Becoming an Imperial Power

The Spanish-American War was a critical event that led the United States to reconsider its foreign policy. In 1898, American newspapers told stories that many people in Cuba suffered from Spain's oppression. Public support for the American involvement in Cuba increased, and President

William McKinley decided to enter a war with Spain. The United States won the war, taking control over Cuba, Puerto Rico and the Phillipines from Spain. The Spanish-American War was the first armed conflict with a European country other than England that Americans had experienced. The war made the United States reexamine the principles of its foreign policy. Rather than abolishing the Monroe Doctrine, the foreign policy vision was revised.

The Monroe Doctrine not only sought to prevent European countries from intervening in the American continents. It also shaped the role the United States played in the continents. It allowed the United States to hold a unilateral policy toward the Latin American countries. Moreover, it reconfirmed that the New World – the American continents – was different from the Old World and that the United States should keep the New World "new" by supporting the American founding principles.

The Progressive Presidents – Theodore Roosevelt, William Taft, and Woodrow Wilson – sought to justify America's expanding involvement in Latin America under the Monroe Doctrine. Roosevelt became famous for his idea that in foreign policy the United States should "speak softly and carry a big stick." With this "big stick diplomacy," he claimed that the United States should use its military power against the Latin American nations to protect the national interest. In 1903, for example, he ordered the U.S. Navy to assist Panama, part of Columbia, to rebel and gain independence. Having a canal for large ships in Panama shortened time for commercial ships and naval vessels to go to the Pacific Ocean from the Atlantic Ocean. For Roosevelt, making the canal by military force was critical for the American interest.

While Roosevelt emphasized the military power, William Taft after him stressed that the federal government should encourage the private sector to invest in foreign countries for American business and the national interest. A major foreign policy objective of the United States abroad was to make better economic and political environments for American business.

This idea was characterized as "dollar diplomacy." It paved the way for "Banana Republics" in Latin America. The United States would support coercive regimes in Latin American countries as long as they were friendly to American corporations like the United Fruit Company. These companies exploited workers in those countries to produce exotic fruits, like the banana, which was then sold back in the United States to American consumers.

President Roosevelt running an American steam-shovel at Culebra Cut, Panama Canal, by Underwood & Underwood publishers (1906). Courtesy of the U.S. Library of Congress.

After Taft, Woodrow Wilson sought to add ethical and moral aspects to American diplomacy. He claimed that American diplomacy was not only about military power and capitalism, but also about political ideology. More specifically, he argued that the United States should not be part of the European power game and that the United States as the leader of democracy should play a role in civilizing people in the developing countries and spreading democracy to those people. His idea is called "missionary diplomacy."

All three approaches justified, at least in the United States' view, the involvement of the United States in Latin America. But all of them, consciously or not, opened the door for the United States to intervene outside the American continents. Its first move in this direction was in the Philippines.

During the administrations of the progressive Presidents, the United States had colonial authority over the Philippines as a result of the Spanish-American War. The Monroe Doctrine provided little guidance about the American role there. The acquisition of the Philippines caused a heated controversy because it looked like a radical departure from the traditional American foreign policy, for two reasons. First, the Philippines were not in the western hemisphere, and thus fell outside of the geography that the Monroe Doctrine assumed. Second, the acquisition of the Philippines meant that the United States had gotten involved in European politics and imperial ambitions. By that time, Britain, France, Holland, and other European powers already had colonies in Asia.

As the United States became an economically developed country by the end of the nineteenth century, however, it was more and more interested in the Asian region and especially China for commercial and financial purposes. The three approaches – military, capitalist and ideological – supported the expansion of federal government capacity to intervene abroad and covered it with legitimacy as it got involved in the Asian region.

Roosevelt's expansion of the Navy allowed the federal government to have the capacity to get involved in Asia. As private business went to China, according to dollar diplomacy, the federal government was urged to support them. Finally, missionary diplomacy justified how the United States entered China not to oppress the Chinese people but to civilize them. Although, military expansion, dollar diplomacy and civilizational missions helped to guide and justify movement into Asia, it was still difficult for the federal government and the American people to accept such a clear departure from the isolationist policy that had guided the nation for more than a century.

World War I

The American role in World War I marked a clearer departure from the Monroe Doctrine. But at the beginning of the war, the Monroe Doctrine made the United States hesitate to enter the war. When the war broke out in Europe, Woodrow Wilson declared the neutrality of the United States. The Monroe Doctrine affected Wilson's decision to remain isolated from European politics while maintaining the economic interactions with all countries in Europe entering the war.

But Germany's surprise attacks on two ships – the Lusitania and the Sussex – killed and injured civilians and angered the American public.

Several other factors pushed Wilson to enter the war. The public in general had more sympathy for Britain, which shared a common political culture with the United States than it had for Germany, governed by an authoritarian regime. Finally, as the war advanced, it became clear that the war would end more favorably for the Allies if the United States entered the war and that otherwise, the United States would be in danger of Germany's attack. Wilson declared war against the Axis countries and justified the decision as "an act of high principle and idealism" and a "crusade to make the world safe for democracy."

Wilson's use of missionary diplomacy rhetoric became a serious challenge to the Monroe Doctrine. A major shift came when Wilson proposed that the United States should be part of the League of Nations. The formation of the League of Nations was presented in Wilson's Fourteen Points for Peace: "A general association of nations must be formed under specific covenants for the purpose of affording mutual guarantees of political independence and territorial integrity to great and small states alike." It was formed as a result of the Paris Peace Conference in 1919 as the first international organization to seek world peace.

Although the United States was now seen as a possible leader in the world, many American politicians back in the United States did not want the United States to take a new leadership role on the global stage. The Senate rejected Wilson's idea by two-thirds of its votes. Many Republicans particularly opposed Article X of the Covenant of the League of Nations. It stipulated that the members were obliged to defend their fellow countries if they were under attack, which meant that the United States would be permanently involved in international politics. The Senate defined the American engagement in WWI as a temporary measure and claimed that the United States should go back to the Monroe Doctrine.

Despite the rejection of the League of Nations, the United States could not entirely retire from international affairs given its involvement in World War I and its enduring presence in Asia. The United States was now a major military power that affected the military situation of the globe. It was also a major economic power that had stakes all over the world and kept interested in the Asian region. With this increased military and economic power, the United States stayed in international politics.

The Washington Conference was an example. The United States proposed the conference and Japan, Britain, France and Italy attended. The Conference produced the Five-Power Naval Limitation Treaty to introduce naval arms control and establish an international order, especially in the Pacific region. The limits on the number of capital ships owned by the United States, Britain, Japan, France, Italy were decided according to the ratio of 5:5:3:1.67:1.67. The United States was interested in the Treaty to prevent further crunches on the American military, but the Treaty also meant that the United States would continue to be enmeshed in world politics.

World War II and the Cold War

In 1931, the Manchurian Incident took place and it became clear that Japan's involvement in China challenged the international order sought by the Washington Conference. The United States was again reluctant to enter the war. Neutrality Acts were passed in 1930s to ensure that the United States would not be dragged into the international conflicts. But as the war advanced more and more favorably for Germany, the Lend-Lease Act was passed to allow the United States to sell the war materials to the Allies. Then Japan's attack on Pearl Harbor in December 1942 made the United States formally enter the war. The United States again fought the world war but its engagement in international politics was drastically changed by WWII.

World War II ended with the American victory. After the war, the United States never completely came back to the Monroe Doctrine. Even before the war ended, the United States took decisive actions to engage with other countries in the postwar world. The United States with Britain and Soviet Union met at the Yalta Conference in February 1945 and

Crimean Conference--Prime Minister Winston Churchill (left), President Franklin D. Roosevelt, and Marshal Joseph Stalin (right) at the palace in Yalta, where the Big Three met, by U.S. Signal Corps photo (1945). Courtesy of the U.S. Library of Congress.

Potsdam Conference in July 1945 to discuss the new institutions to create a new international order. Unlike American opposition to the League of Nations after WWI, moreover, the United States this time joined the United Nations and promised its permanent engagement in international affairs. After the United States began to play a central role in the international community, the question became how the United States should engage in world politics. The idea of big-stick diplomacy, dollar diplomacy, and missionary diplomacy affected the foreign policy. However, the Monroe Doctrine did not disappear and continued to echo behind the policy debate.

If one compares the American situation with the Japanese one, he or she can understand better the domestic and international contexts the United States were in after the war. Japan lost the war and the U.S.-led occupation took place in Japan. Many social, economic and political institutions were demolished; many government officials were purged; and Japan had to accept the new Constitution drafted by the occupation authority. Japan lost its voice in the international community. Then as the Korean War occurred, the United States asked Japan to have the National Policy Reserve which later became the National Defense Forces. Finally, when the Francisco Peace Treaty came into force in 1952, Japan was enmeshed in the United States' strategic foreign policy. Retrospectively, the divergent paths the Japan and the United States took was amazing because before the war both countries were rising-star countries in the eastern and western worlds. Because the United States won the war, it could maintain the core foreign policy principles and have a luxury to define its foreign policy by itself.

However, the United States could not have total control over world politics after the war. Immediately after the war, the Cold War became intense and the United States had to counter the Soviet Union's communist vision. The United States offered aids to rebuild and stabilize the economy of its allies in Europe and Asia, including Japan, and ultimately brought prosperity to American business. The United States played a leading role as a protector of capitalism and democracy, though it focused more on advancing the interests of American business than supporting democratic development in other nations. In fact, when these two goals came into conflict in many countries around the world, especially in the Middle East and in Latin America, the United States often allowed its national economic interests to prevail. Meanwhile, as the ideological conflict between capitalism and communism endured, the United States kept outpacing the Soviet Union in a race to produce more powerful armaments, including large nuclear arsenals.

The Korean War (1950-53) and the Vietnam War (1955-1975) were major "hot wars" in the Cold War. Based on the domino theory that if one country falls in the communist camp its neighbor countries will follow it, the United States sent its military to defend capitalist governments abroad, even when they were not democratically supported.

After the United States became bogged down in the Vietnam War, Henry Kissinger who served under Richard Nixon as a national security advisor and Secretary of State brought a new concept to American foreign policy that drew upon the old European concept of balance of power diplomacy. Through what is called his "realist approach," which takes the balance-of-power among major counties more seriously than moral idealism and political ideology, Kissinger opened talks with communist China to prevent the Soviet Union from further expanding its power. But in contrast to Kissinger's view, President Jimmy Carter argued that human rights considerations should be the center of American foreign policy. His idea recalled Wilson's missionary diplomacy and Carter sought to gain moral supremacy over the Soviet Union.

The New Era after the Cold War?

The Cold War ended when the Soviet Union collapsed. It seemed that the United States has become the sole victor. As Figure 13 shows, American military power is dominant. The American defense budget in 2011 was the largest in the world and more than the amount combined from the second to the tenth countries. The American GDP was also the largest in 2011. It was more than the combination of the gross domestic product (GDP) of the second (China) and the third (Japan). However, the American victory in the Cold War brought new difficulties to the United States.

First, while the possibility of large-scale military conflicts is much less now than it was during the Cold War, smaller conflicts occur more often. There have been

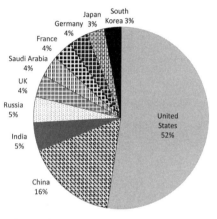

Source: SIPRI Military Expenditure Database

Figure 13: The 10 Counties with the Highest Military Spending in 2011 (US$ Billion)

many ethnic and religious conflicts within countries across the world. Congo and Rwanda. The foreign policy question for the United States was how it should react when human rights violations, such as genocide, occur. Another difficult problem for the United States is terrorist organizations such as Al Qaeda and ISIS that operate across national borders. There is not a clear victory in the "war on terror." But the United States has to continue the endless war on terror as long as terrorist threats to the United States exist.

Second, the rise of China makes it hard for the United States to have a consistent foreign policy. The economic ties with China have become deeper and deeper, and many American companies rely on China for their production, sales, and investment. In this sense, the United States has to coexist with China for its business interests. On the other hand, China has not improved its human rights record as much as the United States hoped. Moreover, China has been expanding its military power. For all these reasons, the United States stands in opposition to China.

Third, given its super economic and military power and given the legacy of the Monroe Doctrine, the United States has often been tempted to act alone in international affairs and for its interests, which is called unilateralism. A unilateral approach was demonstrated in the case of the War in Iraq, when the United States did not ask for the support from the North Atlantic Treaty Organization (NATO) and the United Nations. But without a clear worldwide confrontation like the Cold War, it is difficult for the United States to have its own way without approval from its allies.

In this new environment, the United States looks for a new foreign policy principle beyond the Monroe Doctrine, big-stick diplomacy, dollar diplomacy, missionary diplomacy, and balance-of-power diplomacy. President Barack Obama promised to change George W. Bush's foreign policy by trying to adopt a multilateral approach. But his efforts to communicate with others have often been contradicted by the reality of American foreign policy.

Donald Trump clearly saw the contradiction and suggested a different vision. His foreign policy was called "America First." His core target was working-class voters in the Rust Belt. The workers used to be afford having nice houses and sending kids to universities, but their salary has been significantly decreased, and they do not see American dream as a reality anymore. To respond their frustration, Trump did not expand redistribution policy but work against globalization, multilateralism, and expanding influence of China. Trump lost the election in 2020, but his legacy remained in the Biden administration. The Biden sees the economic security is national security and frames his foreign policy as "foreign policy for middle class."

The United States does not have a financial power and political will to be a global policeman anymore. On the other hand, China has 4 times higher population than the United States and will have more economic and military powers. What the United States will come out of Trump's policy legacy is important for the future of peace in the world.

Cross-Cultural Dialogue 13: War and the People

Michael : "I lived in New York City from 2002 to 2004, when the George W. Bush administration was beginning to beat the drum for war in Iraq. During the lead up to the war, which started in March 2003, Bush dispatched his Secretary of State, Colin Powell, to the United Nations to present evidence that Saddam Hussein's regime in Iraq was secretly building weapons of mass destruction. The evidence was very thin. An international weapons inspection team declared it was highly unlikely that Iraq had such weapons. I wrote a letter to my Senator – then Hillary Clinton, the wife of the former President and later the Secretary of State in the Obama administration – urging her not to give authority to the Bush administration to use military force. She, along with most of the Senate voted to authorize that force, and the Bush administration went to war, which it had seemed determined to do all along. Hundreds of thousands of Americans opposed the war and huge protests occurred in the streets of New York and Washington, D.C. None of that stopped the war from happening, and more than a trillion dollars later, the American intervention there has just become another chapter in our interventionist foreign policy history. I think one of the most painful experiences a citizen can go through is watching his country fighting a bad or unjust war. I would guess the situation is different in Japan."

Taka : "To the Japanese, your frustration is very American. Under Article 9 and the current interpretation of the constitution, Japan cannot send troops to rogue nations by just claiming that they have weapons of mass destruction that would possibly target Japan. Therefore, some Japanese say that whether Iraq had weapons of

mass destruction or not, the United States is selfish to intervene in other nations. I have been to many war museums and memorials in the United States. I can see how Americans memorialize wars is different from the Japanese way. While Americans more likely remember World Wars and other wars as 'necessary wars' to advance the idea of freedom and democracy, Japanese tend to remember the past wars rather in terms of what the country should not have done. I think in addition to the differences in the constitutions of Japan and the United States, the difference in memorializing process also makes it harder for Americans and Japanese to fully understand what others are thinking about when incidents, like war in Iraq, took place."

Further Readings to Study American Politics
アメリカ政治をさらに勉強したい人のための文献

日本語（アメリカ政治全般に関するテキスト）

岡山裕、西山隆行『アメリカの政治』弘文堂、2019年

久保文明『アメリカの政治史』有斐閣、2018年

齋藤眞、古矢旬『アメリカ政治外交史』東京大学出版会、2012年

佐々木卓也編『戦後アメリカ外交史』（第3版）有斐閣、2017年

English (More detailed readings on American politics)

David T. Canon, John J. Coleman, Kenneth R. Mayer eds. *The Enduing Debate: Classic and Contemporary Readings in American Politics*, 8th edition (New York: W. W. Norton & Company, 2017)

Richard J. Ellis and Michael Nelson, eds. *Debating Reform: Conflicting Perspectives on How to Fix the American Political System*, 4th edition (Washington, D.C.: CQ Press, 2020).

Theodore Lowi et al., *American Government Power and Purposes*, 6th edition (New York: W. W. Norton a Company, 2021)

James Morone and Rogan Kersh, *By the People: Debating American Government* (New York: Oxford University Press, 2020).

Acknowledgements
謝　辞

We would like to thank many people who made completion of this book possible. Yoneyuki Sugita at Osaka University encouraged us to write the book, went through all the chapters and gave us valuable comments as we finalized it. We also would like to thank Mamoru Sato and Ai Yasuda at Daigaku Kyoiku Shuppan for their support to publish our book. Lastly, we must thank the Nagoya American Studies Summer Seminar and Nanzan University which hosted the international conferences from 2007 to 2011. We met at one of the five conferences in 2009. We would like to extend our appreciation to Presidents Hans-Jürgen Marx and Michael Calmano, and other faculty and staff members for giving us such wonderful opportunity, which lead us to do this project. This book reflects the spirit of the conference: international scholars working together to study the United States from comparative perspectives. Errors and omissions are our own fault.

Takakazu Yamagishi: I would like to thank my former mentors, Fumiaki Kubo, Adam Sheinagte, and Matthew Crenson. Their intelligence, passion, and openness to new thinking have definitely contributed to this book. I appreciate the financial support for this project by the Pache Research Subsidy I-A-2 for Academic Year 2021 from Nanzan University and Grant-in Aid for Scientific Research (A) (B). In addition, I extend a big thanks to my colleagues and students at Nanzan University. Thanks to them, my time at Nanzan University has been wonderful. Particularly, I owe the idea for this book to the former students in my American politics seminar, what is called "Yamagishi Zemi," who struggled to do my assignments yet demonstrated their great ability. Their stragge pushed me to write this book. Junko Ito and Sachiko Nishimura, my research assistants, also helped me to complete this project. Lastly, I would like to mention my family. Without the great cheerleaders – my wife Yuka, and our sons Chikara and Kazushi – I would not have been pursuing my academic career and this book could not have been completed.

Michael Callaghan Pisapia: I want to thank my academic mentors at the University of Wisconsin, Madison, and especially John Coleman, who encouraged my participation in the Nagoya American Studies Summer Seminar at Nanzan University. In addition, I thank the organizers of that conference, whose hospitality will never be forgotten. I would also like to thank the Political Science Department at Elizabethtown College and the Dean of Faculty there, Fletcher McClellan, for their support of my research presentation at the Social Science History Association conference in Boston, MA. Going to that conference led me to touch base again with Taka. I also want to thank the Department of Politics and International Affairs at Wake Forest University for welcoming me to Winston-Salem, NC in the summer of 2012, and for supporting my work on this project. Finally, writing this book would not have been possible without the time, love and energy that my wife Page gives to our family, and to raising our beautiful children Sophia, Darian and Amalia. We look forward to visiting Japan together someday soon.

シリーズ監修者

杉田　米行
すぎた　よねゆき

執筆者紹介

山岸　敬和 （Yamagishi Takakazu）

1972年、福井県生まれ。南山大学国際教養学部教授。慶應義塾大学修士課程修了。ジョンズ・ホプキンス大学博士課程修了。政治学博士。ジョージタウン大学客員研究員（2011年9月〜2013年3月）。主要業績：『激動のアメリカ—理論と現場から』（大学教育出版、2021年12月刊行予定）（共編著）、『ポスト・オバマのアメリカ』（大学教育出版、2016年）（共編著）、『アメリカ医療制度の政治史—20世紀の経験とオバマケア』（名古屋大学出版会、2014年）、*War and Health Insurance Policy in Japan and the United States: World War II to Postwar Reconstruction* (Johns Hopkins University Press, 2011)，

Michael Callaghan Pisapia
（マイケル・カラハン・ピサピア）

Born in Rio de Janeiro, Brazil in 1978. Assistant Professor, Department of Politics and International Affairs, Wake Forest University. Ph.D. in political science from the University of Wisconsin-Madison. Major publications: "*Public Education and the Role of Women in American Political Development, 1852-1979*." Ph.D. dissertation (won the American Political Science Association's 2011 William Anderson award); "The Authority of Women in the Political Development of American Public Education, 1860-1930." *Studies in American Political Development* (2010).

AS シリーズ 第 8 巻

American Politics
from American and Japanese Perspectives　2nd Edition
——英語と日米比較で学ぶアメリカ政治——

2013年 4 月20日　初　版第 1 刷発行
2021年 9 月30日　第 2 版第 1 刷発行

■著　　者—— 山岸敬和・Michael Callaghan Pisapia
■発 行 者—— 佐藤　守
■発 行 所—— 株式会社 **大学教育出版**
　　　　　　〒700-0953　岡山市南区西市855-4
　　　　　　電話(086)244-1268(代)　FAX(086)246-0294
■印刷製本—— モリモト印刷㈱

ISBN978-4-86692-153-2